DESIGN AND MAKE

CURTAINS

HEATHER LUKE

For Peter

———

This edition published in 1997 by
New Holland (Publishers) Ltd
London • Cape Town • Sydney • Singapore

24 Nutford Place
London W1H 6DQ
United Kingdom

80 McKenzie Street
Cape Town 8001
South Africa

3/2 Aquatic Drive
Frenchs Forest, NSW 2086
Australia

ISBN 1 85368 526 7 (hb)
ISBN 1 85368 527 5 (pb)

Managing Editor: Gillian Haslam
Editor: Coral Walker
Designers: Kit Johnson and Roger Daniels
Photographer: David Johnson
Illustrations: Lizzie Sanders

Editorial Direction: Yvonne McFarlane

Typeset by Ace Filmsetting Ltd, Frome, Somerset
Reproduction by Hirt and Carter (Pty) Ltd
Printed and bound by Tien Wah Press, Singapore

ACKNOWLEDGEMENTS

My thanks to Sarah Westcott, Julie Troop and Jackie Pullman for their expert making up,
to Michael and Don for their on-site help, David Johnson for the brilliant photographs
and the team whose inspiration and magic have made the raw materials into a book -
Yvonne, Gillian and Coral at New Holland. Special thanks to Mary Stewart Wilson,
Elizabeth Peck, Heather Phelps Brown and Jano Clarke for allowing me to show you
some 'vignettes' of their lovely homes.

We would like to thank the following suppliers for their help:
Osborne and Little for the fabrics on pages 27, 34, 37, 42, 57, 61 top left, 68.
Pierre Frey for the fabrics on pages 53, 62, 72 and the photograph on page 55.
Designers Guild for the photographs on page 18.
Mulberry page 51 bottom right.
Byron and Byron for the fittings on pages 43 top left, 46 right, 60 bottom right, 76.
Wemyss Houles for the fittings on pages 27, 53, 66, 74.
Artisan for the fittings on pages 39, 43 top left and top right, 54, 58, 62 top, 63.
Merchants for the fittings on pages 27, 54.

CONTENTS

INTRODUCTION

Layers of vibrant silk organza are ruched and draped to create a dramatic and exciting window treatment with a minimum of sewing skills.

Whether motivated by pleasure or necessity, most of us at some time in our lives choose to make our own curtains. While first-time projects are propelled by adventure, novelty and enthusiasm, later homemade curtains can all too often be relegated to secondary rooms as we turn instead to a professional to handle the more important ones. However, it is these areas of the home which can give the curtain-maker the greatest satisfaction. Indeed, making curtains can be dull, but adding the element of 'design' to the task of making, elevates the project from the mundane to something exciting, absorbing and fulfilling.

In this book, I have brought together a mixture of designs; both rooms and windows which I have been commissioned to decorate, and window treatments which I have conceived and made specially for this book. Your own situation might be perfect for one of these designs, but my aim is to encourage you to create your own treatments, details and finishes.

Any window treatments you choose should reflect the period of your house and the style of your furnishings. If you feel unsure about mixing colours, textures and patterns, stay with the colours with which you feel most comfortable, but approach them in a new way. Collect scraps of fabrics and coloured papers, study books and magazines so that you can begin to understand just how colours work together and how you could use different combinations, patterns and textures. For example, red and yellow used with orange could be quite ghastly or very exciting, depending entirely on the tone of each colour. (The tone explains the amount of white added to the pigment; so a colour is described as light, medium or dark. The hue explains the intensity, for example, the amount of green and blue which create the colour aquamarine.)

DESIGN AND MAKE CURTAINS

Single colour or monochromatic schemes are created using tones and hues of the same colour. A good example is to think of a summer garden and to examine the number of different greens that sit comfortably together. Relate this theory to any colour: mix mauves, coral, raspberry and strawberry ice cream colours together under the banner 'pink'. Two-colour or related colour schemes are based on colours which are compatible. For example, use blue and green as separate colours in varying tones mixed with hues of blue-green and green-blue. Most schemes will also employ a complementary or accent colour, that is, a colour from the opposite side of the spectrum. Add a touch of red to blue and green, for instance.

Neutral mixes can be mouth-wateringly successful if you remember there is a whole range beyond the usual white, cream and black. Try the earth colours of sand, butter, stone, and brick with brass, steel, limed wood, dark oak or palest ash.

Texture, too, plays a vital part in your choice of fabric and in the way that a particular colour will look in situ.

Use ideas from contemporary and historical fashion, but always avoid 'trends' which might date your curtains. Classic fabrics and colours, perfectly made into curtains with detailed finishes which complement the overall room design, will stand the test of time. Of course, you may wish to change your curtains often and I have suggested simple and inexpensive ideas to accomplish this.

BASIC TECHNIQUES

STITCHES

Always ensure you start and finish all stitching with a double stitch, never use a knot.

Hemming stitch

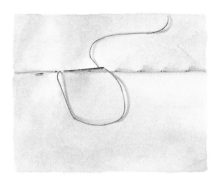

This stitch is used along the hems of lined curtains and the hems and sides of unlined curtains. Each stitch should be approximately 1.5 cm (⅝ in) in length. Slide the needle through the folded hem, pick up two threads of the main fabric, and push the needle directly back into the fold.

Herringbone stitch

Herringbone stitch is used over any raw edge which is then covered by another fabric. It is worked in the opposite direction to all other stitches. So right handers will work from left to right. Each whole stitch should be approximately 3 cm (1¼ in) for hems (a) and 8 cm (3¼ in) for side turnings (b). Stitch into the hem, from right to left, approximately 1.5 cm (⅝ in) to the right make a

a
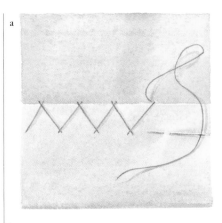

b
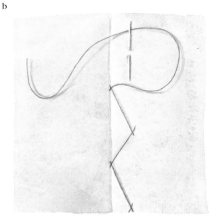

stitch into the curtain picking up two threads. Pull through and stitch 1.5 cm (⅝ in) to the right, making a stitch into the hem.

Ladder stitch

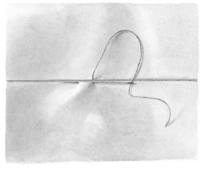

Ladder stitch is used to join two folded edges invisibly together. Slide the needle along the fold 5 mm (¼ in) and straight into the fold opposite. Slide along for 5 mm (¼ in) and back into the first fold, again directly opposite.

Long stitch

Long stitch is the most effective stitch to hold the side turnings of interlined curtains as it holds the interlining tight to the main fabric. Make a horizontal stitch approximately 1 cm (⅜ in) across. Bring the thread down diagonally by about 4 cm (1½ in) and repeat.

Slip stitch

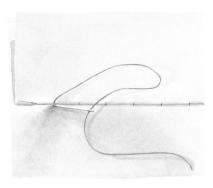

This stitch is used to sew linings on to curtains. Always use a colour thread which matches the main fabric. Make each stitch approximately 1.5 cm (⅝ in). Slide the needle through the main fabric and pick up two threads of the lining. Push the needle back into the main fabric exactly opposite and slide through a further 1.5 cm (⅝ in).

Lock stitch

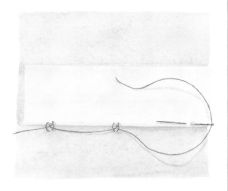

This stitch holds linings, interlinings and fabrics together, preventing them from separating, but still allowing some degree of necessary movement. Always use thread that blends with the background of the curtain fabric and the lining colour when stitching lining to interlining. Fold back the lining, secure the thread to the lining and make a small stitch in the main fabric just below. Make a large loop approximately 10 cm (4 in) long (slightly shorter for small items, like pelmets) and make a small stitch in the lining inside this loop. Stitch into the main fabric. Do not pull the stitch too tightly, but allow it to remain slightly loose.

Buttonhole stitch

Used of course for buttonholes, but also wherever a raw edge needs to be strengthened or neatened. Work from left to right with the raw edge uppermost. Push the needle from the back to the front, approximately 3 mm (1/8 in) below the edge. Twist the thread around the needle and pull the needle through, carefully tightening the thread so that it knots right on the edge of the fabric to form a ridge.

Blanket stitch

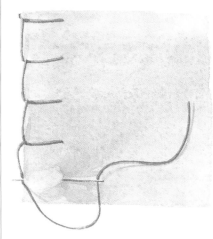

Originally used to neaten the raw edges of woollen blankets, its use is now mainly decorative. It is most comfortable worked from the side with the edge towards you. Push the needle from the front to the back, about 6 mm (1/4 in) from the edge (this measurement will vary with large or small items). Hold the thread from the last stitch under the needle and pull up to make a loop on the edge.

PINNING

When pinning two layers of fabric together or piping on to fabric, always use horizontal and vertical pins to keep the fabric in place from both directions. The horizontal pins need to be removed just before the machine foot reaches them and the vertical ones – or cross pins – can remain

in place, so the fabrics are held together the whole time.

SEAMS

Flat seam

The most common and straightforward seam for normal use. With right sides together, pin 1.5–2 cm (5/8–3/4 in) in from the edge at 10 cm (4 in) intervals. Pin cross pins halfway between each seam pin. These cross pins will remain in place while you are stitching to prevent the fabrics slipping. Once machine-stitched, open the seam flat and press from the back. Press from the front. Now press from the back, under each flap, to remove the pressed ridge line.

French seam

Use for sheers and unlined curtains or any occasion when the seam might be visible.

Pin the fabrics together with the wrong sides facing. Stitch 5 mm (¼ in) from the raw edges. Trim and flip the fabric over, bringing the right sides together. Pin again, 1 cm (⅜ in) from the stitched edge and stitch along this line to enclose the raw edges. Press from the right side, always pressing the seam in one direction only.

Flat fell seam

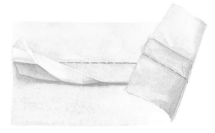

Use for neatening seams of heavier weight fabrics. Pin the fabrics together with the right sides facing and stitch 1.5–3 cm (⅝–1¼ in) from the raw edges. Trim one seam to just under half. Fold the other over to enclose the raw edge. Press down. Stitch close to the fold line.

MITRED CORNERS

When sides and hems are equal

1. Press the side seam over and the hem up. Position a pin through the point of the corner.

2. Open out the folds and turn in the corner at a 45° angle, with the pin at the centre of the foldline.

3. Fold the hem up and the sides in again along the original fold lines. Keep the pin on the point and make sure the fabric is firmly tucked into the folded lines.

When sides and hems are unequal

Follow step 1 as above, but when you reach step 2, the corner will not be folded to a 45° angle.

Instead, the corner of the fold will need to be angled away, towards the hem, leaving a longer fold on the side turnings so that the raw edges meet when the mitred corner is finished.

MAKING TIES

Ties are both useful and decorative and are used extensively throughout soft furnishings. For curtains, they are used primarily to tie a heading to a ring or pole. They are also used for tying cushion sides, seat pads and fastening loose covers.

Folded ties

Cut a strip of fabric four times the width of your finished tie and 3 cm (1¼ in) longer.

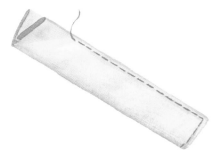

Press one short end under by 1 cm (⅜ in). Press in half lengthwise, fold each side to the middle, press, fold and stitch close to the folded edges.

Rouleau ties

Cut a strip of fabric four times the width of your finished tie and 3 cm (1¼ in) longer. Fold in half lengthwise, right sides together, enclosing a piece of cord which is longer than the strip of fabric. Stitch along the short side to secure the cord firmly. If the rouleau is quite wide, knot the cord as well. Stitch along the

length, 2 mm (⅛ in) towards the raw edge from the centre.

Trim the fabric across the corner, pull the cord through, at the same time turning the fabric right side out. Cut off the cord at the end. Press the raw edge under and slipstitch with small stitches.

PIPING

If piping is to be used in straight lines then it will be easier to cut it straight. If it is to be bent around corners, then it should be cut on the cross. For 4 mm (⅛ in) piping cord cut 4 cm (1½ in) wide strips. All joins should be made on the cross to minimise bulk when the fabric is folded.

To cut on the straight

Cut lengths as long as possible. Hold two strips, butting the ends together as if making a continuous length. Trim away both corners at a 45° angle. Hold together and flip the top one over. Stitch where the two pieces cross.

To cut on the cross

With the fabric flat on the table fold one bottom corner as if making a 30 cm (12 in) square. Cut along the fold line. Mark pencil lines from this cut edge at

4 cm (1½ in) intervals, and cut along these lines. Hold two pieces butting the ends together as if making a continuous strip. Flip the top one over and stitch together where the two fabrics cross.

Making up and pinning on

Press seams flat and cut away excess corners. Fold in half along the length and insert the piping cord. Machine stitch to encase, approximately 2 mm (⅛ in) from the cord. Keep the fabric folded exactly in half.

Always pin piping so that the raw edges of the piping line up with those of the main fabric.

To bend piping around curves, snip into the stitching line for the piping to lie flat. For a right angle, stop pinning 1.5 cm (⅝ in) from the corner, snip the piping right to the stitching line, fold the piping to 90° and start pinning 1.5 cm (⅝ in) on the adjacent side.

Joining

To join piping, overlap by approximately 6 cm (2¼ in). Unpick the casing on one side and cut away the cord so that the two ends butt up. Fold the piping fabric across at a 45° angle and cut along this fold. Fold under 1 cm (⅜ in) and pin securely before stitching.

BINDING

Binding one edge

1. Cut the binding strips to the width required (I use 1.5 cm (⅝ in) as an average.) Join the strips – always on the cross – to make the required length.
2. Pin the binding to the fabric, right sides together and stitch 1.4 cm (slightly less than ⅝ in) from the raw edges.

3. Neaten the raw edges to 1.4 cm (slightly less than ⅝ in). Press from the front, pressing the binding away from the main fabric. Fold the binding to the back, measuring the edge to 1.5 cm (⅝ in), keeping the fabric tucked firmly into the fold and pin at 8 cm (3¼ in) intervals. Turn to the back and herringbone the edge of the binding to the main fabric.

Binding a corner

Stop pinning short of the corner by the width of the finished binding. Fold binding back on itself to make a sharp angle and pin across this fold line. Pin on the adjacent side, the same distance from the edge. Stitch binding on, stopping at the pin and secure. Begin stitching again at the same point on the adjacent side. Press to mitre. Fold fabric to the back, mitring in the opposite direction.

UNUSUAL WINDOWS

Not all windows are neat-and-tidy rectangles or squares, set into a vertical wall. Irregular windows always tax the designer's imagination, how to dress them without spoiling the shape, where and how to hang the fittings. And how do you tackle windows set into sloping eaves? Try some of these ideas if you have a less than ordinary window shape.

Simple wooden buttons (right) do not take away from the window shape and could be painted to match the wall exactly. The voile can be hung to one side or right across with little effort.

I originally devised the method of 'curtaining' (far right) to cover hexagonal windows in an attic guest bedroom in Holland and have used this idea many times since. I think it is the perfect

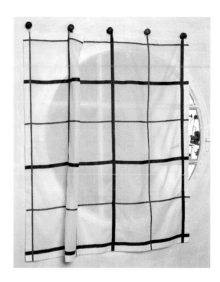

DESIGN AND MAKE CURTAINS

solution for almost any unusual window shape and for windows which need only little or occasional covering. The line of the frame is completely un-disturbed, the cover could be left either attached to the lower hooks or folded away when not in use.

Traditional curtains would have taken too much light from my bathroom (below left), so I had a swing metal frame made which sits back against the wall in the daytime and closes over each window at night.

Sloping windows are a recurrent problem with attic conversions. We chose primary colours to decorate this teenage girls' bedroom (right) and painted the poles to match the beds. Blue checked gingham tied back with unfinished strips of fabric cut on the cross provided just the right crisp, but informal, foil to the busy and colourful wallpaper.

A first-floor bedroom in a barn conversion left me with these problem windows (right). My brief was to create a romantic, feminine room from a vast space, so we first covered the walls in a fabric reminiscent of a cottage garden, specially printed for us in France, and then canopied the bed in silk and lace. I designed overlong silk curtains with bunched headings tied back to frame the wonderful woodland outlook. Sash ties with bows and lace under-curtains add the necessary feminine touches and reflect the bed canopy. A roller blind covered to match is discreetly hidden behind the heading during the day and is quick to pull down at night to keep out the dark and cold.

CURTAIN FITTINGS

CURTAIN TRACKS

For most uses, metal tracks with plastic runners and an enclosed pull-cording system are the best. These tracks are available in several different qualities to suit the weight and length of your curtains and are easily adaptable to 'top fit' on to a pelmet board or into the recess, or to 'face fit' to the wall, to a batten or directly on to the window frame. They are also available in telescopic lengths to suit a range of window sizes. You can also buy small tracks specifically for sheer curtains which often need to be fitted invisibly behind a pole or into a space behind the main curtains.

Cording is essential to protect interlined and long curtains. Attach cord weights which are heavy enough to keep the cords taut, and fit S clips to prevent them twisting. You might prefer to have a pulley system fitted which will keep the cords running in a continuous loop.

Side fittings, which hold the track to the wall, are available in several different sizes so that the track can be fitted either very close to the wall or some distance out. This facility allows the curtains to hang straight over a radiator or deep sill.

TRACK COVERS

Tracks are best unseen, so make a track cover to disguise the fittings. Cover it in the same fabric as the curtains or paint it to blend in

with the wall. Make the top with wood and the front with plywood. The brackets will need to be housed into the wood to allow the fabric cover to fit neatly.

Cover the top, front and inside of the board with interlining and then the whole item with fabric. Starting at the back, work across the top, down the front and

inside. Glue only in three places – at the back on the topside and the underside, and inside where the 6 mm (¼ in) front joins the board. Fit to the wall and camouflage the centre bracket and any side brackets with wallpaper or paint.

PELMET BOARDS

Pelmet boards need to suit the quality and weight of the curtaining and pelmets. Always add sides and fronts to the pelmet board to keep the pelmets from brushing against the curtains and to prevent the pelmet tipping backwards. Use wood for the top and 6 mm (¼ in) plywood for the front, with substantial brackets to hold the weight.

Paint the board to match the

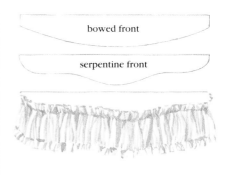

shaped tops

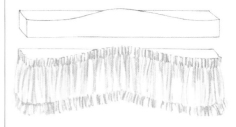

shaped fronts

window frame or cover the whole board with fabric to match the curtains. Ensure the front of the track is fitted approximately 50 mm (2 in) from the front of the board so that the heading can draw freely but without leaving a large gap. For a shaped board, choose a track which will bend to follow the front line.

CURTAIN POLES

There are so many different types of pole and finial style available in the shops that you will be spoilt for choice.

Choose poles which can be fitted as closely to the wall as possible with brackets which have fixings above and below the pole, otherwise heavy curtains could pull the fitting away from the wall. The end brackets should be positioned so that there is approximately 3 cm (1¼ in) from the fitting to the end of the pole, just enough space for one curtain ring. The curtain will then pull right to the end of the pole.

MEASURING AND PLANNING

The most successful window treatments have been carefully considered and designed before the fabric has even been purchased. Once you have taken accurate window measurements (see right) round them up or down to the nearest 5 mm (¼ in) and transfer them to graph paper. If you have neither scale rulers nor graph paper, work with a very simple scale, say, 1 cm = 10 cm or 1 in = 10 in, and a normal ruler.

Mark the room height, the position of the window and the space around the window. If there is a bay, beam or other obstacle, mark this also. Please don't be put off if you have no drawing experience. The examples here are deliberately simple to give you the confidence to try.

You will need tracing paper to place over your window plan and paper clips to hold them together. Experiment by drawing different curtains and fitting positions: long, short, with or without pelmets, formal or gathered headings, etc. You will soon begin to formulate suitable ideas.

Once you have a fairly definite concept, draw the window again, tidying up the measurements and draw the design as accurately as you can. Try to mark exactly where the fittings should be – how far to the side of the window and how far above. If you want to make a pelmet, mark the top,

sides and centre and shape the edge roughly.

Translate your ideas to the window by marking the walls around with a soft pencil and stand back to look. You will need to make an accurate template for a pelmet (see page 74). Most fittings can be cut to size, so ask someone to hold them in place for you to see what they will look like before they are finally fitted.

TAKING ACCURATE MEASUREMENTS

Measure the width and height at least three times so that you are aware if the window is not 'square' and if the floor or ceiling slopes.

Measurements to take
● From the top of the frame or reveal to the floor.
● From the ceiling (or under the cornice) to the top of the window.
● From the ceiling to the floor.
● The window width inside – noting any possible problems, eg, telephone sockets, etc.
● The window width outside.
● Measure the distance available all around the window for the curtain stack-back, avoiding pictures, bookcases, etc.

Stand back and check for any ugly fitments which might need to be covered. Measure and note unsightly double-glazing fittings, odd bits of wood, etc. Decide whether you need blinds and/or pelmets or fixed curtain headings. Plan how – and exactly where – they should be positioned. If a pelmet is to be used, make a template and tape it into position to check how it will look.

For curtains to hang outside reveal

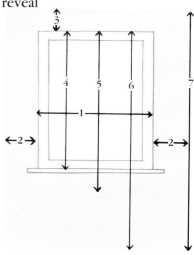

1 width of window
2 width of stack-back
3 top of architrave to ceiling
4 top of architrave to sill
5 top of architrave to below sill
6 top of architrave to floor
7 ceiling to floor

For curtains to hang inside reveal

1 width inside reveal
2 length from top of window to sill
3 depth of reveal

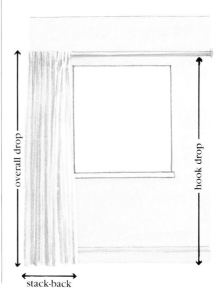

overall drop

hook drop

stack-back

ESTIMATING FOR CURTAINS

HEADING REQUIREMENTS

Heading Type	Fullness Required
Gathered headings	
Tape	1.75 – 2.25
Ties	1.25 – 2.50
Handsewn	2.50 – 3.00
Bunched	2.25 – 2.50
Smocked	2.50 – 3.50
Pencil pleated	2.50 – 2.75
Hand Pleated	
Triple (French)	2.25 – 2.75
Goblets	2.25 – 2.50
Folded	
Pocket	2.00 – 3.00
Voiles	2.50 – 3.00

Most curtains look best with at least double fullness, but this may be reduced for short curtains which do not need the weight to hang well. If stack-back space is restricted, pleated headings will hold the curtain back into the smallest space. Allow only 1¼ to 1½ times fullness for a heavy fabric or one with a dominant design which needs to be seen.

HEADING ALLOWANCES

Bunched
Allow enough for a 10–12 cm (4–4¾ in) 'bunch' depending on the thickness of the fabric. Allow the hook drop plus 25–50 cm (10–20 in).

Frilled
Allow the frill above the hook drop and back to fit under the tape.

Allow the hook drop plus 12 cm (4½ in) for a 6 cm (2¼ in) frill, 16 cm (6½ in) for an 8 cm (3¼ in) frill, etc.

Pencil pleated
Allow the depth of the pleats.
Allow the overall drop plus 6–8 cm (2¼–3¼ in).

Pocket headings
For voiles, allow 2 cm (¾ in) for the pocket and 2 cm (¾ in) above.
Allow the overall drop plus 8 cm (3¼ in).

Bound headings
No allowance needed.
Overall drop, no extra.

Smocked
Allow the depth of the smocking pattern.
Allow the overall drop plus the depth of the smocking pattern.

Goblet/triple pleats
Allow double the depth of the pleat.
Allow the overall drop plus 20 cm (8 in) for a 10 cm (4 in) pleat.
Allow the overall drop plus 30 cm (12 in) for a 15 cm (6 in) pleat.

HEM ALLOWANCES

Unlined curtains	16 cm (6¼ in)
Lined curtains	16 cm (6¼ in)
Lined, bound hems, plain lining	8 cm (3¼ in)
Lined, bound hems, contrast lining	No extra fabric
Interlined curtains	12 cm (4¾ in)
Voile curtains	8–12 cm (3¼–4¾ in)

ESTIMATING FOR FABRIC

The quantity of fabric needed for each window is relative to the style of curtaining which you wish to make. The three factors are: the headings style, the fullness, and the curtain length. You will have already chosen your window treatment style following the guidelines on page 12 and from this you will know the fittings width and the overall drop of the curtains. The hook drop is the measurement from the top of the curtain hook and the bottom of the curtain fitting, to the hemline. The overall drop is from the top of the heading to the hemline. You will need to estimate these measurements from your plan, until the fittings are in position. The overall drop is from the top of the heading to the hemline.

Make allowances for any changes – for instance, if cupboards are to be fitted close to the window, or a possible change of flooring. Use the following as a guide.

EACH LENGTH

1. Find the overall drop

ceiling to floorboards	270 cm	(106 in)
less allowance for carpet of 2 cm (¾ in)	268 cm	(105¼ in)
less allowance for pelmet board of 2 cm (¾ in)	266 cm	(104½ in)
plus overlong hem allowance of 5 cm (2 in)	271 cm	(106½ in)

2. Add the hem and heading allowances

hem	12 cm	(4¾ in)
heading	20 cm (8 in)	
each cut length	303 cm (119 in)	

3. Adjust for pattern repeat, if necessary

If the pattern repeat is 65 cm (25½ in)

303 cm ÷ 65 cm = 4.66
(119 in ÷ 25½ in = 4.66)
round up to 5.

Allow 5 repeats for each cut as each cut length must include complete pattern repeats.

5 × 65 cm = 325 cm
(5 × 25½ in = 127½ in)
Each cut length will need to be 325 cm (127½ in).

Note the fabric 'wastage': 325 cm (127½ in) is needed for each cut, yet only 303 cm (119 in) is actually needed for the curtain, so five pieces of 22 cm (8½ in) will be left.

At this point you can decide how best to use this spare fabric. You might decide to alter the headings, for example to have a frilled and bound heading rather than bound only, or to increase the heading fullness from frilled to bunched. Or this spare could be allocated for tiebacks, pelmets, etc, depending on the amount available.

Fabric pelmets can be very expensive, but can often be cut from the same piece of fabric, with each curtain cut. Another advantage is that the pattern is already matched.

Planning the fabric in this way means that you will never have wasted pieces, and will be aware when cutting of the importance of using the fabric wisely.

If the fabric you have chosen is expensive and the estimated cuts are just over a whole repeat (i.e. 4.1 repeats) you might decide to shorten the hem or heading allowance a little. Just enough to save costs without damaging the hanging quality.

Always allow an extra pattern repeat to the total amount of fabric estimated, to allow you to start your hemline in the position on the pattern which you choose.

HOW MANY WIDTHS

1. Select your fitting and divide the length in half for two curtains

180 cm ÷ 2 = 90 cm
(70 in ÷ 2 = 35 in)

2. Add the side return (10 cm/4 in) and the centre overlap (10 cm/4 in)

90 cm + 10 cm + 10 cm = 110 cm
(35 in + 4 in + 4 in = 43 in)

3. Multiply by the fullness needed for your heading

110 cm × 2.5 = 275 cm
(43 in × 2.5 = 107½ in, say 108 in)

4. Divide by the width of your fabric

275 cm ÷ 135 cm = 2.04
(108 in ÷ 54 in = 2)
Therefore, use two cuts per curtain

5. Multiply the number of widths by the cut lengths

Plain fabric
303 cm × 4 = 12.12 metres
(119 in × 4 = 13¼ yd)
You will need 12.12 m (13¼ yd)

Patterned fabric
325 cm × 4 = 13 metres
+ 65 cm for extra repeat = 13.65 metres
(127½ in × 4 = 14 yd
+ 25½ in = 14¾ yd)
You will need 13.65 m (14¾ yd)

MAKING TEMPLATES

Make accurate templates of anything which might prevent drapes hanging well. Cornices will usually be above the curtaining, but sometimes the side of the pelmet will need to return on to the cornice, there might be a plate rack or picture rail or pipes obstructing the fall of the curtains.

Use brown paper and a pencil to draw around the obstruction, if possible. If not, tear the paper roughly and cut in around it accurately with a sharp knife.

HAND-PLEATED HEADINGS

(Aim for pleats of 15 cm (6 in) and gaps between pleats of 12 cm (4½ in).

For a fitting size of 195 cm (76½ in) each curtain will be
97.5 cm + 10 cm + 10 cm = 117.5 cm
(38¼ in + 4 in + 4 in = 46¼ in)

1. Work out the number of pleats and gaps

97.5 cm ÷ 12 cm = 8.13
(38¼ in ÷ 4½ in = 8½),
say 8 gaps and therefore 9 pleats

2. Work out the fabric needed for the pleats

9 × 15 cm = 135 cm
(9 × 6 in = 54 in)

3. Add this plus side turnings to the curtain width

117.5 cm + 135 cm + 12 cm = 264.5 cm
(46¼ in + 54 in + 4½ in = 104¾ in)

4. Divide this by the fabric width

265 cm ÷ 135 cm = 1.96
(104¾ in ÷ 54 in = 1.92)

So, round up to allow two widths of fabric for each curtain.

If this calculation had worked out so that there was spare fabric in the widths, you could increase the size of the pleats to accommodate, or to cut away the excess. Conversely, if the fabric requirement calculated that you would only just need to cut into a full width, you could use slightly less fabric in each pleat.

If your room has two or more windows which vary in width, all curtains will need to have exactly the same size pleats and distance between pleats. In this case the widths will need to be cut down to exact measurements for each curtain.

PREPARATION

This is the key to successful sewing. Prepare well, and the work should go smoothly, with few errors. Look at various factors before you begin: where you are going to work, what you plan to work on, the fabric you plan to use, linings and interlinings. Here are some guidelines to bear in mind before you begin sewing.

THE WORKTABLE

If possible, you should stake your claim on one room which can be put aside for your own use, even if it is only while you are making your curtains.

A dining room or guest bedroom can be made into a temporary workroom with little effort. A worktable which is at least 2.5 × 1.2 m (8 × 4 ft) and preferably 3 × 1.5 m (10 × 5 ft) will make the whole job so much easier. You can buy a sheet of board in either of these sizes. Cover your dining table with thick felt so that the board can be rested safely on top.

Alternatively, make some sturdy legs which can be bracketed on to the underside of the board. This quickly made table can then be fitted temporarily over a guest bed. The space below can be used to store all your fabrics, linings and interlinings and the top will be wide enough for you to work on a whole width of fabric at a time. Pure luxury compared to hands and knees on the floor!

The height of the worktable should be whatever is comfortable for you; I use a table that is 95 cm (38 in) high.

Cover the top with heavy interlining and then a layer of lining. Staple these to the underside; pulling the fabrics very taut as you go. You will now have a soft surface which is ideal for pinning and pressing.

CUTTING OUT

Before you begin to cut the fabric, check it thoroughly for flaws. Try to cut around simple line flaws or incorporate them into headings and hems. If the fabric is badly flawed, return it.

Measure out each length and mark with pins to make sure that you have the correct amount of fabric. Always double check your measurements before cutting.

Fabric should ideally be cut along the grain and to pattern, but sometimes the printing method allows the pattern to move off grain. Make sure that the leading edges of all pairs of curtains match exactly. If necessary, allow the pattern to run out slightly to either side – but a 2 cm (¾ in) run-off is the most you should tolerate. Do not be tempted to follow the pattern and cut off the grain, as the curtain edges will not hang straight. As you cut each piece, mark the right sides and the direction of a plain fabric just in case there is a weave variation which is not noticeable until the curtains have been made up and hung.

Try not to fold your lengths at all, but if you do need to fold them, make sure it is always lengthwise. We have a series of poles fitted to the wall of the workroom over which each length is hung until it is ready for use. You might have a bannister rail which could serve the same purpose.

Join the widths and half widths as planned, using flat seams for all lined and interlined curtains (see page 7), French seams for lightweight unlined curtains (page 8), and flat fell seams for heavy unlined curtains (page 8).

PATTERN MATCHING

It is well worth spending a little time to make sure that all fabric patterns are matched correctly at the seam on each width. Curtains which are otherwise well made can easily be let down by cutting corners at this stage.

1. Place one of the lengths of fabric right side up on the worktable with the selvedge facing you. Place the next length over the first, right side down. Fold over the selvedge to reveal roughly 5 mm (¼ in) of pattern and press lightly.

2. Match the pattern to the piece underneath, and pin through the fold line along the whole length. You may need to ease one of the sides at times – using more pins will help. Go back and place cross pins between each pin. Machine or hand stitch along the fold line, removing the straight pins and stitching over the cross pins.

3. Press the seam from the wrong side and then again from the front. Use a hot iron and press quickly. Turn the fabric over again to the back and press under the seam to remove the pressed ridges. If the background fabric is dark or you are using a woven fabric, snip into the selvedges at

5 cm (2 in) intervals. If the background fabric is light, trim the selvedges back to 1.5 cm (⅝ in), removing any printed writing.

FABRIC WITH BORDERS

Some fabrics have printed or woven borders on one or both sides, so before cutting you need to determine where and how to use them. When the border is on both sides of the fabric, decide whether the border should appear on the leading and outside edges only, or whether one border should appear at each seam, in which case the extra border should be removed as the widths are joined.

I often prefer to remove the centre borders completely and use the extra lengths to allow the border to continue along the hem and 'frame' the curtain.

Where there is a border on one side of the fabric only, it should appear on the leading edge of each curtain. You will need to trim the border from the whole length and stitch it back on to each leading edge. Do check whether the border has a directional pattern and make sure that you pin it back on accordingly.

PREPARING LININGS

Cut out your lining fabric as closely to the grain as possible. Because this is often hard to see, allow about 5 cm (2 in) extra for each cut length.

Join lining widths with flat seams. If your curtains have half widths, it is easier to join all whole widths first and then cut the centre width through the middle. This avoids the possibility

of making up two left or right linings rather than a pair. Press all seams to lay open.

To make up the hems, place one lining on to the worktable, wrong side facing up, with one selvedge exactly along the edge of the table. It is unlikely that the cut line will be exactly straight, so turn up approximately 12 cm (4½ in) along the lower edge and press in place. Keep this folded line parallel to the bottom of the table. Trim the hem to 10 cm (4 in) from the fold and then fold it in half to make a 5 cm (2 in) double hem. Pin and machine stitch close to the fold line or slipstitch by hand.

INTERLININGS

It is important that interlining is cut out following the grain. If it is not stitched into the curtain exactly square, after a period of time it will fall down into the hemline. Use the grain line at headings and hems to help you.

Join all widths with flat seams and trim them back to 2 cm (¾ in), snipping into the selvedge at 5 cm (2 in) intervals.

WEIGHTS

To ensure that curtains hang and drape well, you should insert weights into curtain hems at each seam and at each corner. Make a lining cover for each weight to prevent it rubbing and possibly discolouring the fabric. Very heavy curtains or sheer curtains should have a length of fabric-covered chain weight threaded into the hem instead. Chain weight is available in different weights to suit all purposes.

DRESSING CURTAINS

Hand-headed curtains need to be dressed as soon as they are hung so that the pleats are trained to fall evenly. You will need to leave the curtains tied back for at least 48 hours and possibly up to 96 hours. The waiting will be well rewarded as your curtains will always hang well.

Begin by drawing the curtains to the stack-back position. Make sure that the heading is in order, the pleats are forwards and the gaps are folded evenly between each pleat. If the curtain hangs under a track or pole, the gaps will fold behind, if in front, the gaps will fold to the front.

Stand at eye level with the headings and take each pleat, smoothing it down through the curtain as far as you can reach to form a fold. Now, standing on the floor or lower down the step ladder and starting at the leading edge, follow these pleats through to waist height. From the leading edge fold each pleat back on to the last. Tie a strip of fabric loosely around the curtain to hold the pleats in place.

Kneel on the floor and follow the folds through into the hem. Finger press firmly. If the curtains are overlong, keep the pleats together and bend the curtain to one side. Tie another strip of fabric around the curtain hems to hold the pleats in place, loosely enough not to mark the fabric, but tight enough so that they do not slip down.

Springy fabrics may need to be readjusted several times, but this will become easier as the pleats are trained.

UNLINED CURTAINS

Unlined curtains are the simplest
form of window covering to make
and, with careful preparation and
well chosen fabric, your curtains
can look as good as any more
complicated design. For those
new to curtain-making, this is the
place to start. If you need to make
something quickly or perhaps find
yourself on a very tight budget,
unlined curtains using inexpensive
fabrics but with plenty of fullness
will make effective and very
rewarding window treatments. I
often use unlined curtains as draw
curtains for the summer, allowing
the sunlight to filter through while
the heavier winter curtains are
draped up to the sides.

Use silks, muslins, calicoes, and
experiment with ribbons, braids,
cords, ties, buttons and motifs to
produce your own personalised
finish. Turn to pages 40 – 47 to
see how very good sheers and
layered curtains can look.

**Change heavy winter curtains to
simple unlined cotton for the summer
months. Crisp blue and white edging
defines these white curtains and
coordinating tablecloth.**

MAKING UP

1. Place the cut and joined fabric for one curtain on to the worktable, with the right side facing down, lining up the hem and one side with two edges of the table. Smooth the fabric out, sweeping the edge of a metre rule or yardstick across the table and press to remove any creases. Turn in the side edge by 6 cm (2¼ in) using a small measuring gauge to make sure that the turning is even. Press lightly. Fold in half to give a 3 cm (1⅛ in) double turning. Pin and press again. Turn up the hem by 10 cm (4 in). Press lightly, then fold in half to make a 5 cm (2 in) double hem. Pin and press.

2. For medium to heavyweight fabrics, mitre the corner as shown here and described more fully on page 8.

3. Stitch both the sides and the hem with neat slip stitches, 1.5–2 cm (⅝–¾ in) in length. Ladder stitch the corner, slipping in a fabric-covered weight.

4. For sheer and lightweight fabrics, fold the sides and hems over so that the layers are exactly on top of each other, and slip stitch along the fold so that the stitches are almost invisible.

5. Measure from the hem to the top of the curtain to mark the hook drop of the finished curtain. If you do not yet have the exact measurements because the fittings are not in place, mark the estimated position. Measure at 30 cm (12 in) intervals and pin a line across the curtain. If you know the overall drop also mark this line with a row of pins.

6. Carefully move the curtain across the table and repeat with the other side.

7. Sheer, unlined curtains which will be used in doorways or open windows will need to be weighted along the hems to prevent them flapping about in any breeze. Insert a length of fabric-covered chain weight (see page 17) into the hem.

8. An attractive alternative to step 7 is to stitch several rows of decorative stitching to give the required weight and substance to the curtain hem.

LINED CURTAINS

The purpose of lining curtains is twofold – firstly, to protect the principal fabric from exposure to sunlight and/or the effects of condensation which will eventually cause fading and rotting, and secondly to add bulk.

Cotton sateen lining is available in three basic shades – ecru, cream and white, and in various qualities. A specialist furnishing fabric supplier will also be able to offer you coloured linings so that you can tone your lining with the main fabric. Lining fabric is relatively inexpensive and my advice is always to buy the best lining possible. If you look at several different qualities, you will immediately see the difference in the weight of yarn and quality of weave, and realise that saving costs on the lining fabric will be a false economy.

It is important that the lining you choose has been treated to withstand strong sunlight and dampness. However, while good curtain fabric will last for many years, linings should be replaced completely every 10–15 years. A window with a sunny aspect will need more linings and curtains than a north-facing window. Once a year, check the linings and replace the leading edge as soon as it starts to wear.

Lining curtains adds body as well as protecting the main fabric from the effects of strong sunlight or dampness. Over-sized gathered headings flop over informally.

DESIGN AND MAKE CURTAINS

MAKING UP

1. Place the fabric for one curtain on the worktable with the right side facing down, lining up the hem and one long side to two edges of the table. Smooth out the fabric and press to remove any creases. Turn in the side seams by 6 cm (2¼ in), using a small measuring gauge to make sure that the turning is even. Pin every 12–15 cm (4¾–6 in) and press. Turn up the hem by 16 cm (6½ in), checking that the pattern runs evenly across the width, and press lightly. Open out the fold and refold in half, to make an 8 cm (3¼ in) double hem. Pin and press.

2. Mitre the corners as shown here and described more fully on page 8. Make an angled mitre so that the hem and the side match along the diagonal.

3. Stitch the length of the side with herringbone stitches, approximately 5 cm (2 in) in length. Picking up only one thread at a time, slip stitch the hem, stitching a weight into each seam. Ladder stitch the mitre, slipping a weight into the corner.

4. Place the pre-prepared curtain lining (see page 17) on top of the curtain, wrong sides together, matching the seam lines and placing the top of the lining hem exactly on top of the curtain hem.

5. Turn back the lining and lock stitch to secure the lining twice across each width at equal distances and at all seams, using the same colour thread as the lining fabric. Reposition the lining and smooth out the creases.

6. Using scissors, score the lining along the folded edge of the curtain. Trim along this line. Turn the raw edge under leaving 3 cm (1¼ in) of curtain showing. Pin and stitch the edges of the curtain beginning 4 cm (1½ in) from the bottom corner and continuing until just below the heading.

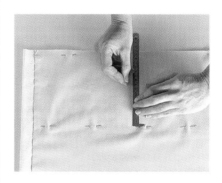

7. Measure from the hem to the top of the curtain and mark the hook drop of the finished curtain. If you cannot be exact because the fittings are not in place, mark the estimated position. Measure across the curtain at 30 cm (12 in) intervals and pin through both layers along the hook drop line. Mark the overall drop line with pins.

8. Fold the side to the middle and move the curtain across the table. Make up the other side in the same way.

INTERLINED CURTAINS

These curtains were made with unbleached artists' canvas, laundered first to take up the shrinkage and lined with a fine cotton pinstripe ticking. A mediumweight, cotton interlining was chosen to add enough body and weight to help hold back the leading edges and reveal the linings.

Apart from the practical advantages of offering additional insulation to your home – interlined curtains look and feel sumptuous and luxurious. These types of curtains always fall in generous folds and can be dressed to pleat back formally or to gather informally.

Light-flowing fabrics can be transformed into elegant drapes by first stitching the fabric to heavy interlining, allowing the body and weight of the interlining to hold the top fabric. Interlining linen or heavy cotton curtains for doorways and windows in country cottages and farmhouses will keep any draughts and cold from the room – much more effective and less expensive than double glazing or additional heating!

Interlining is available in several different weights, so you should choose the weight best suited to your needs. It is not necessary to put heavy interlining with heavy fabric and light with light – in fact, the opposite can transform a very lightweight fabric.

Always ask to test a length of interlining against your fabric. Hold fabric and interlining up together and see how the natural drape of the fabric is affected before you decide to buy.

Most interlinings are 90% cotton twill woven with approximately 10% of other fibres and brushed to encourage the fabric to hold heat. An interlining made wholly with manmade fibre is readily available, much less expensive and, although not as effective as the cotton interlining, is very light to work with, making stitching and handling easier.

MAKING UP

1. Place the fabric for one curtain on the worktable with the right side facing down, lining up the hem and one long side to two edges of the table. Smooth the fabric out, sweeping the edge of a metre rule or yardstick across the table. Clamp the fabric to the table at approximately 60 cm (24 in) intervals. Place the interlining on top, lining up the seams and hems and smooth out as before.

2. The interlining must now be locked to the main fabric at each seam and twice between each seam. Fold the interlining back on itself at the first seam and lock stitch all the way down using double thread. Stitch close to the hem but stop just short of the hook drop. Fold the interlining back flat, smooth out and then fold two thirds back again. Repeat the lock stitch for the whole length and again on the third of the width.

Your curtain is likely to be wider than your table; however, as interlined curtains should not be moved until they are stitched together, you must finish this part of the curtain before moving the other half on to the table.

3. Trim the interlining if necessary so that the sides of both the main fabric and the interlining are even. Remove the side clamps and turn back both fabric and interlining by 6 cm (2¼ in), using a small measuring gauge to make sure that the turning is even. With the tips of your fingers, check that the interlining is well tucked into the fold and a solid, firm edge is pinned in place. (A soft fabric might require the interlining to be locked to the main fabric along the folded edge. Use small stitches and make sure that they do not pull on the fabric at all.)

Trim the interlining along the hem if necessary and fold it up by 12 cm (4¾ in). Press lightly and pin securely.

4. Mitre the bottom corner following the instructions on page 8. Make a long mitre so that the 12 cm (4¾ in) hem and the 6 cm (2¼ in) side match along the diagonal. If you are using very heavy interlining with heavy fabric you might need to cut away the bulk of the interlining. Open out the mitre and trim along the folded diagonal line.

5. Stitch along the length of the side with long stitches approximately 5 cm (2 in) in length as shown on page 6 and along the hem with 2 cm (¾ in) herringbone stitches. Catch both layers of interlining but do not go through to the front fabric. Insert a weight into the mitre opening and ladder stitch to close with small, neat stitches.

6. Clamp the curtain back on to the table. Place the lining over the interlining, matching up the seam lines and allowing the lining to overhang the hem by approximately 10 cm (4 in). Smooth out with the ruler and lock the lining to the interlining along the same lines that hold the interlining to the main fabric. Start at the hemline and finish just before the hook drop.

DESIGN AND MAKE CURTAINS

7. With the point of the scissors, score the lining along the folded edge and trim to this line. Fold under the raw edge, leaving 3 cm (1¼ in) of the curtain fabric showing. Pin to secure. Trim the hem of the lining so that it is exactly 10 cm (4 in) longer than the curtain. Pin the lower, raw edge to the hem fold and take up the excess fabric by finger pressing a tuck into the lining along the stitched hemline. Press this fold downwards and pin to hold it in place. Fold the raw edge of the lining under so that the fold is 4 cm (1½ in) from the hem. Pin. Slip stitch the sides and hem from the hook drop to the edge of the table.

8. At this stage, measure from the hem to the top of the curtain to mark the hook drop of the finished curtain. If you do not yet have the exact measurement because fittings are not in place, mark the estimated position. Measure across the curtain at 30 cm (12 in) intervals and pin through all three layers at the hook drop measurement, to secure. Pin two or three more times between each of these to make a definite line.

9. Remove the clamps and carefully lift the curtain along the table. You should ask for some help to do this, so that the fabrics are disturbed as little as possible.

Re-clamp the other side of the curtain to the table. Continue smoothing the interlining against the main fabric, folding it back and locking in as before. Mark the hook drop all along to line up with the other side.

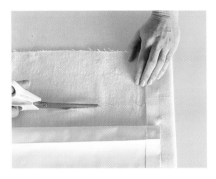

10. Check the exact overall drop measurements and mark with pins accordingly. Fold the lining back on itself along the pinned line. Remove the pins and carefully cut away the interlining along this line. Pin again to secure. Herringbone stitch the interlining to the curtain. Fold the main fabric over with the lining and continue with your chosen heading.

OVERLONG CURTAINS

The choice of curtain hem length is a purely personal one, however I usually advise and make curtains just 2–3 cm (¾–1¼ in) longer than floor length so that the fabric just bumps the floor. The reasons for this are several. Firstly, curtain fabric can drop or pull back in the time between making up and hanging, thus making it very difficult for an amateur to gauge an exact length. Secondly, very few window tops are parallel to the floor and overlong curtains make this variation less obvious. Old houses will almost always have draughts from around the window frame and below the skirting boards, which overlong curtains take up. And last, but by no means least, I *like* the look of curtains which just fall to the floor.

HEADINGS

A little spare fabric has been used to make alternately coloured tabs which, together with self-covered buttons, provide a striking and contemporary heading. Make your own tabbed or tied heading by following the step-by-step instructions on page 34.

Headings need to be both practical and decorative. Usually the functional qualities must override the decorative, but there are occasions when the window treatment will be for ornament only and then headings can be embellished with cords and tassels, rosettes and fringes with scant regard to function.

Hand-pleated headings are neat and tidy, suitable for formal window treatments and where the curtains need to pull back into a limited space. Gathered headings suit informal curtaining, as pleats may be pulled up at random and headings tied and buttoned to poles and rings. Hand gathered pleats are formal, especially if hand stitched or smocked. Rich and voluptuous headings can be created with excess fabric – turn into overlong frills flopping to the front of the curtain or scrunch randomly along the curtain top.

Tabbed headings are smart alternatives to any pleating or gathering and give a lovely decorative finish. Unfortunately, the use of these headings is restricted to windows where the curtain pole is easily reached as the headings have to be eased back by hand.

Headings can be finished with an almost infinite variety of detail. Buttons, ribbons, beads and sequins, braided edges, hand stitching and embroidery, contrast fabrics for double and triple frills, binding, backings and edgings, scallops and drapes – any or all to suit your window treatment.

The type of heading you use will depend on a number of factors: the size of the window, the style of the window treatment, whether the curtains need to be well stacked back or can be more decorative than practical.

DESIGN AND MAKE CURTAINS

HAND-PLEATED HEADINGS

Hand pleating encourages curtain headings to pull back evenly, providing a neat finish to the top of any curtains. Stiff heading buckram is used to support hand-pleated headings so that both the pleats and the gaps between keep their shape. Available in a variety of widths, the most useful are 10 cm and 15 cm (4 in and 6 in), both of which can be cut down if necessary. You should be able to buy heading buckram from a furnishing fabric specialist and some department stores. I prefer to stitch the buckram in place as the fusible type does not always stick evenly.

Goblet pleats make a less formal heading than French pleats, but take up more track space when curtains are pulled back.

MAKING UP

1. The hook drop and the overall drop will be the same for these headings. Measure double the depth of the buckram and trim the fabric evenly to this measurement. Fold the fabric over along the overall drop line and press lightly. Lay the fabric flat again, fold back the lining, and trim away the interlining along the pressed line. Herringbone stitch to hold the interlining in place.

2. Place the buckram on the fabric against the cut edge of the interlining and herringbone stitch.

3. Fold the lining back. Fold the fabric over the bottom edge of the buckram and then fold again. Pin along and slip stitch the ends.

4. To position the heading pleats and gaps needed, refer to your plan (see pages 13–15). Measure the flat width of the curtain and deduct the finished width including the overlap and return. Divide the difference between the number of gaps. Keeping the pleat measurement as estimated, mark the overlap, the pleats, gaps, and return, across the width.

5. Fold and pin the pleats firmly in position at the top and bottom of the buckram. Machine down the length of each pleat and fasten securely. Remove all pins. Turn to the front and make pleats.

DESIGN AND MAKE CURTAINS

HAND HEADINGS

1. Triple pleats or French pleats are ideal for a formal finish, under pelmets and where curtains need to be pulled back into a limited space. Finish the pleat with a button covered in a contrast-coloured fabric or bind the top edge for smart detail.

Open out the pleat, place three fingers inside and flatten. Then lift the pleat and pinch in the centre fold. Push down to make three equal pleats. 1 cm (³/₈ in) below the base of the pleat, stitch through the fabric to hold the pleat firmly in place. At the top of the pleat, stitch each piece in position so that it holds its shape.

Stitch across each of the three pleats and through the pleats just above the buckram.

2. Inverted pleats: Use for a contemporary finish and where the headings need to be clean-lined.

Stitch the pleats to fold to the inside of the curtain rather than the outside. Open up each one and press flat. Stitch across the top and down each side.

If stack-back space is limited, make double or triple pleats.

3. Goblet pleats: Taking up more space than triple pleats, goblets are often used for less formal curtains or when curtain headings are fixed. Decorate with knotted rope or gilded cord, or finish the goblet with large buttons, tassels or rosettes.

Open the pleat out fully and run a gathering thread around the base, 1 cm (³/₈ in) below the buckram. Cut a rectangle of interlining, roll it up and stuff it into the goblet to give it a well-rounded shape. Cut the other pieces exactly the same size so that all pleats will be equal.

4. Cartridge pleats: Useful as an 'invisible' heading for fabric with a strong pattern or elegant simplicity which is better not disturbed by a more prominent heading. Use small pleats.

Open the pleats out fully and stuff with rolled up interlining to give a solid round shape. Make sure that the interlining for each pleat is cut and rolled equally.

1

2

3

4

GATHERED HEADINGS

Gathered headings may be a simple frill at the top of the curtain, created by stitching on standard hook tape and pulling the cords, or they may be finished with a variety of details. A 6-8 cm (2¼-3¼ in) frill size is ideal with a pole fitting, as it will cover the bottom of the ring but only part of the pole. Adjust as necessary to suit the curtain fitting which you have chosen.

MAKING UP

For a 6 cm (2¼ in) frill you should have allowed 12 cm (4¾ in) plus 1.5 cm (⅝ in) to go under the tape. Cut away all excess fabric.

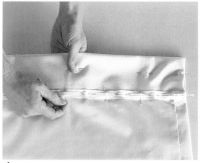

1. If your curtain is interlined, fold the lining back and trim away the interlining at the overall drop line. Fold fabric and lining over, pin on the tape and stitch close to the outer edges, always stitching with the heading towards the body of the machine. Pull the heading up to the required size and gather evenly across the width.

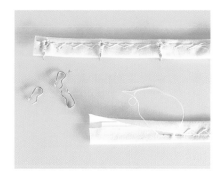

2. Make a hook band. Cut a piece of heading tape or heading buckram the width of the tape and of length equal to the finished heading size. Cut a strip of fabric three times this width and 4 cm (1½ in) longer. Fold the fabric over the band, trimming and herringboning the raw edge. Position hooks at the leading edge, at the return and at 11-13 cm (4¼-5 in) intervals across the width. Stitch securely to the back of the band to cover the tape.

3. Slipstitch the hook band neatly to cover the heading tape.

HAND GATHERED

1. Check your overall drop measurement and adjust pins accordingly. Fold the lining back and trim away the interlining, if used, along the overall drop line. Trim fabric and lining 7.5 cm (3 in) from this line and press to the back. Experiment with different stitch lengths to determine the stitch length you will need to obtain your required pleat size.

2. Divide the heading into 10 sections and mark each with a coloured tack. Make one row of stitches 3 cm (1¼ in) from the folded edge. Make a parallel row 3 cm (1¼ in) from the first. Pull up the two threads together evenly.

3. Make a hook band; divide into sections and match to the heading. Even out gathers, pin and slip stitch.

The binding for headings should be taken from a mid-tone in the fabric.

1. Tied and gathered: As an alternative to hooks, a pretty gathered or pleated heading might be tied to the pole or to curtain rings. Ties could be short and tied into a neat bow, or long and trailing. Plan the number of ties to be about 11–15 cm (4¼–6 in) apart and to suit the pole width. Divide the curtain by this number of gaps between ties and mark the tie positions. Make ties as on page 8 and pin under the tape. Secure each tie with double stitches as the tape is being stitched in place.

2. Scalloped frill: Check your overall drop and hook drop and adjust the pins accordingly. Make a scalloped template, pin this shaped edge along the overall drop line and cut around it through all layers. Using the same template, cut a facing from a strip of main fabric the length of the heading × the frill depth, plus 1.5 cm (⅝ in) to fit under the tape. Make up enough piping (see page 9) and stitch around the scallops. Pin the facing on with right sides together and stitch just

inside the previous stitching line. Trim, snipping into the corners. Press the scallops to shape. Pin and stitch the tape in place and cover with a hook band.

3. Adding ribbon: Check your overall drop and hook drop and adjust the pins accordingly. Add the frill depth plus 1.5 cm (⅝ in) to go under the tape and trim away all excess fabric. Trim away interlining along the overall drop line. Fold over the main fabric and lining and press. Turn the curtain to the front and position the ribbon so that it will finish just 1 cm (⅜ in) from the frill fold. Pin to the fabric only and stitch along both sides. Fold the frill over again and stitch tape to the hook drop measurement. Pull up, spreading gathers evenly and attach the hook band.

4. Pocket headings: Pocket or slot headings allow curtains to be threaded directly on to the pole or wire. They are often used for voiles and sheers and for curtains with a fixed heading which open on to ties or holdbacks rather than being pulled open and closed in the conventional manner. Allow 8–12 cm (3¼–4¾ in) for a curtain frill and 2 cm (¾ in) for voiles above the pocket.

Check your overall drop and trim away any interlining along this line. Add the frill return and twice the pocket depth, and trim away any excess fabric. (To find the pocket depth, add 10 per cent to the circumference of your pole for easement and divide in half.) Fold under, pin and then stitch along both the fold line and the stitching line which will become the top of the pocket.

BUNCHED HEADINGS

Bunched headings are very effective and extremely simple to make. And you can achieve very different looks using this same technique. For example, silk curtains finished with bunched headings look extremely sophisticated, yet heavy linen curtains with the same treatment will look very relaxed and have more of a country style.

Fine fabrics can be bunched successfully if at least three times the fullness of fabric has been used. Insert a length of scrunched organdie or fine net into the heading after the tape has been stitched on to give the curtain body and to help the folds fall correctly.

All interlined curtains make suitable candidates for bunched headings, but if medium or lightweight interlining has been used, insert a double layer into the heading before bunching.

Check the overall drop and hook drop, adjust the pins accordingly. Add the frill depth plus 1.5 cm (⅝ in) to go under the tape and cut away any excess fabric. Trim the interlining back another 2 cm (¾ in). Fold the heading down to the hook drop line, pin and stitch 3 cm (1¼ in) deep tape in place. Pull up and stitch on the hook band.

Turn the curtain to the front and bunch up the heading with your fingers. Using a long needle and double thread secure through the folds and into the back as often as needed to hold the shape without squashing the folds. Sew up the open ends by hand, gathering slightly.

Gathered headings are scrunched up and stitched in place. Hanging from a painted pole, they add an informal finish to these interlined curtains.

TABBED AND TIED HEADINGS

I used a little spare fabric to make alternately coloured tabs and buttons for a checkerboard effect; bought tapes or ribbons could be substituted if your time is limited. Most fabrics respond well to contrasting detail; striped and checked fabrics worked together, with perhaps a plain tone to add definition, are especially rewarding.

None of these headings is difficult to make if you have basic skills and like to experiment with cords, eyelets, ribbons, and even string, to create an individual finish. Some of the headings will not allow the curtains to be pulled back as far as you might wish, but they are ideal for decorative and fixed curtains. Most will allow the curtain to take up little space when pulled back, especially those threaded on to poles through large eyelets.

Always stiffen the headings with buckram, cotton heading tape or dressmakers' interfacing, to prevent the fabric flopping and looking untidy. Hand or machine stitch between the fabric and lining before binding, or insert into a folded heading. Unlined curtains will need a facing to cover the stiffening.

MAKING UP

1. Make fabric tabs in any size, but usually 2–4 cm (³⁄₄–1¹⁄₂ in) wide and long enough to fit easily over your pole. Allow enough for buttoning to the front and fixing to the back. Stitch securely to the curtain heading just beyond the overall drop before turning the heading over.

2. Stitch buttons to the front, securing them right through all layers of fabric. Use strong buttonhole thread to make sure that the tabs are secure, as this stitching will be holding the full weight of the curtain.

DESIGN AND MAKE CURTAINS

1. Add a 5 cm (2 in) border to the top of the curtain and stiffen it with heading buckram. Fit 20 mm (¾ in) eyelets to thread on to a 15 mm (⅝ in) pole.

2. Add 10 cm (4 in) to the overall drop, fold this in half and insert a 5 cm (2 in) band of stiffening; slip stitch along the fold. Punch 10 mm (⅜ in) eyelets and thread through double cords.

3. Add a 5 cm (2 in) border to the top of the curtain and stiffen with heading buckram. Fit 20 mm (¾ in) eyelets and 30 cm (12 in) ribbons to tie to the pole with little half bows.

4. Bind the curtain all round, stitching in 5 cm (2 in) of interfacing into the heading. Make ties measuring 1 × 45 cm (⅜ × 18 in). Stitch into the binding at regular intervals and tie to the curtain rings.

5. Bind the curtain all round, inserting 5 cm (2 in) soft interfacing into the heading. Cut tabs and bind these to match. Secure to the back of the heading and hold the front with a button.

6. Bind the curtain all round, inserting a soft interfacing into the heading. Stitch 100 cm (40 in) ties into the headings at intervals. Loop over the pole and tie in bows.

7. Add 10 cm (4 in) to the overall drop, fold in half, inserting a 5 cm (2 in) stiffening. Stitch 45 × 5 cm (18 × 2 in) piped tabs at regular intervals, loop over the pole and tie into half bows. Stitch in place.

8. Make a stiffened band with a shaped lower edge, the finished width of the curtain. Gather the curtain on to the band. Stitch ribbon loops, fold the band over and decorate with bought motifs.

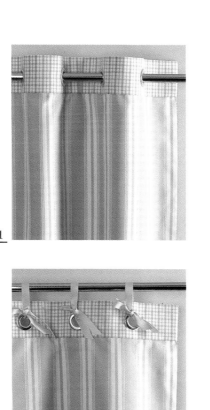

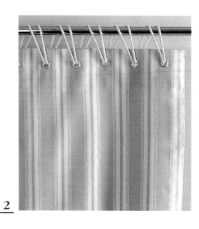

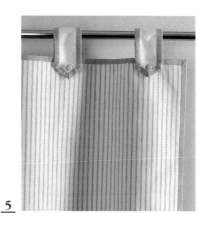

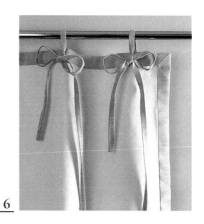

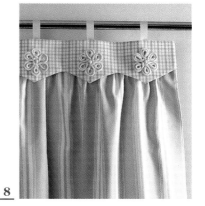

TIEBACKS AND HOLDBACKS

Decorate your fabric tiebacks with fresh flowers and greenery from the garden to match the table decorations for a summer party or a wedding meal.

Tiebacks need to be both practical and decorative, which makes them quite challenging to design and make.

First, choose a style which is in sympathy with your house and window treatment – a formal room will respond best to classic tiebacks, a muted colour scheme will need subtle tiebacks, while a pretty feminine room will be enhanced with bows and frills.

You will discover that tiebacks and holdbacks can also resolve many window dressing difficulties. Problems which I encounter time and again are curtains which, of necessity, hang too near a bathroom or kitchen sink, curtains in front of doors or where both curtains and maximum light are needed at different times of the day.

Many beautiful tiebacks can be bought 'off the peg' or made to order from a wide selection of trimmings (passementerie). Single or double tassels, cord loops or knotted ropes are just some suggestions. Brass and wooden arms or holdbacks are also available. Some will lie flat against the wall when not in use and twist around to hold the width of the curtain edge when needed.

Experiment with these and other ideas – use scarves or belts, add shells or wooden beads, and experiment with mixing fabrics – prints and checks, damasks with fine stripes. Imaginative use of paper, silk or dried flowers can look very attractive, while real flowers and greenery can also decorate curtains for a special occasion.

To measure for tiebacks, hold a tape or piece of rolled up fabric around your curtain. Lift the leading edge of the fabric and drape it to sit into the tieback in a gracious sweep. If the tieback is too loose it will keep slipping up and you will loose the drape, too tight and the fabric will crease and spoil the leading edge.

Fit tieback hooks in pairs, with the outer hook level with the outer edge of the curtain and the inner hook approximately 5 cm (2 in) inside. Tiebacks should have a brass ring sewn on to the inside, approximately 3 cm (1¼ in) in from the front edge, and a 5 cm (2 in) fabric loop to the back edge.

When the curtains are drawn, lift the tieback from the front hook only and let it fall flat behind the curtain. To tie your curtains back, pick the tieback up from behind the curtain and take it around to the front. Try to make this method a habit so the tiebacks remain the right way round and receive a minimum of handling.

Holdbacks will be fitted straight on to the wall or into the wooden frame. Hold the fitting at the edge of the curtain and pull back to the side to establish the best position for the holdback.

Formal and classical tieback fittings should be fitted approximately two thirds down whereas frilled and less formal ties can be fitted at almost any position complementary to the window treatment. Ask someone to hold your curtains back at several different points so that you can choose the hook position.

FABRIC TIEBACKS

MAKING A SASH

To establish the length of the sash, drape a length of scrap fabric around your curtain, trim to size, tie a bow or knot to the front or side of the curtain, pin in position and mark where the rings should be stitched to fit the tieback hook.

Cut fabric the length and twice the width of your template, fold in half with right sides together and stitch from each end to the centre, leaving a 12 cm (4¾ in) gap. Trim the seams back to 5 mm (¼ in), turn through, press and slip stitch the opening. Cut this length into two as shown, turn under the raw edges and pleat the sash ends to approximately 3 cm (1¼ in). Stitch to neaten and stitch a ring just inside one end and a fabric loop in the other. Fit on to the hook and tie into a bow or knot. Stitch so that the bow or knot cannot easily be undone.

Large bows and sashes for feminine window treatments can be made simply and quickly or in much more detail with contrast linings, pipings and ribbons.

MAKING A BOW

To make this bow, cut two pieces of fabric 45 × 12 cm (18 × 4¾ in) and piping to go all round. Stitch the piping to the right side of one piece, very close to the piping stitching line. Place the other piece of fabric over the top, pin carefully in place and stitch from the first side, keeping your stitching line just inside the last one. Leave a 12 cm (4¾ in) gap in the middle. Trim the seams to 5 mm (¼ in) and turn right side out. Pull the corners out with a pin and press along the seam line. Slip stitch the gap, pin the bow to the worktable and tie. Stitch the bow in position so that no one can come along and untie your beautiful creation.

DESIGN AND MAKE CURTAINS

MAKING A ROSE

Use different lengths and widths of fabric for different sized roses and buds. For this rose, cut one piece of fabric 1 m (1 yd) long, making it 14 cm (5½ in) at one end and 10 cm (4 in) at the other. Fold in half lengthwise and run a hand-stitched gathering thread 1.5 cm (⅝ in) in from the raw edges. Pull up to 50 cm (20 in) and, starting at the narrow end, roll up to make the rose, keeping the raw edges tight together. Stitch through all layers to hold the shape, cut a small square of fabric and stitch to the back to cover the frayed ends.

TIES

Simple ties also make very effective tiebacks, again for informal rooms. Tie a piece of tape or an offcut of fabric around your curtain to determine the length and width and follow the instructions on page 8. Checks and stripes can be bought inexpensively and are most effective used on the cross or in complementary colours and different weaves.

ROULEAUX

To make a rouleau measuring 45 × 6 cm (18 × 2¼ in) cut a strip of fabric 50 × 14 cm (20 × 5½ in) and a piece of polyester wadding 50 × 70 cm (20 × 28 in). Roll up the wadding and loosely herringbone. Press under 1.5 cm (⅝ in) along one length. Fold this strip over the wadding roll, pin the folded edge over the raw edge and slip stitch. Cut two small pieces to stitch over the ends, with a ring at one end and a fabric loop at the other.

A rouleau tieback (above) is decorative and is finished with rose in the same fabric. Below: the simplest treatments are so often the most effective.

LINENS AND SHEERS

Floaty drapes, in silk taffeta and muslin, allow maximum light into the room as well as framing the country-side view. Roller blinds keep out the darkness at night and pull up out of sight during the daytime behind a fabric-covered pelmet board.

Sheers encompass unlined and semi transparent curtaining which, although decorative in detail, is chosen and fitted for protection of some sort. Whether to give privacy, to block out excess sunlight, to cover exposed windows, to be 'dirt catchers' in a large city, or as under-curtains which can be used without the main curtains during the summer.

Fabrics used for sheets include muslins, very fine calicoes, organdie, silks, fine linens, linen scrim, lace and cotton voile. Any sheer fabrics used should be easy to clean and should not react to sudden changes in temperature.

Usually white, cream or off white, some linens and cottons can be bought unbleached and muslins, silks and voiles will all dye easily. Specialist furnishing and dressmaking fabric shops will be able to supply ready dyed sheers, but you could also dye your own. Last year, I needed a delicate shade of peachy-pink for a client which proved impossible to source. I solved the problem by steeping four handfuls of raspberry and blackcurrant tea in a bowlful of boiling water for 15 minutes, soaking the muslin for three hours before rinsing away any excess dye and leaving the curtains to dry naturally.

Sheer curtains need to be very full to show the fabric to its best and at least two and a half to three times the fullness for privacy.

DESIGN AND MAKE CURTAINS

1. Curtains are not necessary for privacy in many country situations, but a window dressing and some night time cover may be preferred. Jute scrim, more usually used for cleaning windows, and a fine tea towelling linen were selected for an inexpensive contemporary treatment.

The jute curtain was made with a pocket heading ruched on to a small pole which fitted on cup hooks behind the more decorative steel pole. Cotton ties were stitched into the flat heading of the white curtain and tied to curtain rings. The over-long jute and the floor length white linen add further to the informality of this unusual window treatment.

The gilded star holdbacks are just one example of the variety and fun element in contemporary interior design fittings.

Helpful reference
Pocket headings page 33, ties page 8, overlong curtains page 25

2. Often dark, heavy curtains are perfect for the winter months but feel too heavy if fully drawn throughout spring and summer. One solution is to make two pairs of curtains, the under-curtains only being used in warmer weather.

The sobriety of these main curtains is lightened with the addition of roses on the overlong drape of slubbed silk under-curtains with their fully gathered tape headings and self fabric ties. The outer curtains are completely flat, bound all around in charcoal grey, and lined with dark red. The border was cut from the width and stitched back on to the

leading edge and hem. Brass hooks – hand stitched to the curtain heading at regular intervals – encourage the curtain to pleat back into a very small space.

Helpful reference
Bound edges page 9, roses page 39, borders, pages 56–60, interlined curtains page 22, taped headings page 32, unlined curtains page 18, ties page 8.

3. My studio doors, although copied from a traditional French style, were double glazed, so do not need heavy curtaining, However, I do sometimes need to screen the intense sunlight in the summer when I am working. Steel bars were bent to shape for me by our local blacksmith and I made two flat muslin panels which

Fine linen is a heavier alternative to muslin for under-curtains. Linen is always prone to creasing, but it does filter the light beautifully and the even weave is ideal for hand stitching and to hold the scalloped edges.

double over the bars and slide easily on and off for washing.

The bars can swing back into the recess when the doors are open and to one side whenever the muslin panels are not needed.

4. Sometimes, when a blind is chosen as the preferred window treatment, you may find the window still needs softening. This fabric is most attractive as a flat blind, with the pictures depicting country events from a past way of life. The simple pelmet behind hides the fittings.

To make one the same, measure your window width and divide it into approximately 30 cm (12 in) sections. Add 6 cm (2¼ in) to each section to find the finished width and measure the depth required. Make a rectangle of fabric which is bound along the lower edge and lined. Make ties and buttons, divide the flat fabric into the number of sections needed and stitch the buttons in place, tying the ties around the buttons. Stitch a small brass ring behind each button and fit to small hooks which have been screwed into the window frame at the correct intervals. Finger pleat the hemline to look neat.

The organza curtain was cut 80 cm (32 in) over-long, seamed with French seams, 1 cm (⅜ in) hems were slip stitched all around, and the heading pocketed to ruche on to a wire at the top and tied in a large knot.

Helpful reference
French seams page 8, pocket headings page 33, binding edges page 9, making ties page 8.

1

2

3

4

LAYERS

Two very different linens were chosen for the drapes: inexpensive jute scrim under fine linen, sewn with oversized pin tucks, and hand embroidered in feather stitch.

For the inexperienced, unlined curtains are by far the easiest window treatments to make and probably the most cost-effective, as they save the expense of linings and interlinings.

Easy to store, quick and inexpensive to make, layers of sheer curtains are ideal if you like to change your curtains each season. Unlined, sheer fabrics layer to create some fabulous, eye-catching treatments. Two strong colours such as green and blue or pink and red will vibrate with life and interest, rather like using a fabulous shot silk. Cream and white used together provide a restful, light combination with much more richness and variety than if either colour was used on its own.

There are also other interesting effects you can achieve with layers. A strong fabric, which might in itself be extremely attractive but at the same time a little overpowering, can be 'filtered' by hanging a lightweight voile in front.

The limitations of unlined curtains are that they do not stop draughts, keep out the early morning light or the darkness during the evening. One solution that I employ is to make a blind which hangs against the window frame, providing a 'picture' during the evening in the same manner as the outlook in the daytime. Roman blinds fold up during the daytime and can be interlined to provide some insulation at night. Roller blinds are also effective with layers of sheers as they can be made invisible during the daytime behind a small fitted pelmet board.

1. The printed linen blind against the window called the tune for the colours of these silk organza drapes. White has been used as a foil, with the mid blue ribbon detail picking up the background colour from the blind fabric. The vibrant blue chosen to frame the window reflects the flower centres and has the same ribbon detail, but this time in a toning shade. Thin brass rods were used to thread through the pocket headings of both layers. The outer layer was made with an extra flap of sheer fabric to form an attached pelmet.

Helpful reference

Unlined curtains page 18, pocket headings page 33, pelmets page 70, eyelet headings page 35.

2. Three layers of silk were chosen for their almost clashing tones and the quality of organza which allows each layer to be seen through the other. By shaping the hemlines, the three colours are always on show but the light is always filtered through all three, giving quite a different effect to each layer.

These hems were satin stitched by machine because I wanted the fabric to stretch and ruffle around the curves.

If you enjoy needlework, you might like to shell edge or feather stitch close to the edge.

The headings were all stitched together, ruched on to a narrow metal pole. Two lengths of fabric were wound very informally around a second pole and stitched at each end to tabs, which tie around the pole to hold the drape in place.

Helpful reference

Unlined curtains page 18, pocket headings page 33, pelmets page 70.

3

4

3. Yellow ochre, tan and red layers combine for an exotic effect. The headings of the top two layers were cut into deep scallops and edged with narrow ribbon in complementary colours. By tying each layer back individually, the colours can be seen in their own right and with added depths.

Helpful reference

Unlined curtains page 18, making ties page 8.

4. The whole scheme for this `room was designed from the hand-printed olive leaf chosen for a half blind. Half blinds which pull up and down only a little way are very useful when the outlook from just the top half of a window needs to be obscured. The checked and buttoned edge was later picked up in the sofas and cushions.

The excellent quality of the cloth used for the blind, and the printing technique with its simple design, set a style which I was keen to keep in my interpretation. The walls were coloured and

stencil printed not to copy but to echo the olive leaf design. Two very different linens were chosen for the drapes to reflect the spirit of 'elegant naivete'. The sheers were made from very inexpensive jute scrim and the curtains were made of the best quality linen, sewn with oversized pin tucks and all hand embroidered in feather stitch using perlé thread with a slight sheen which contrasts beautifully and subtly with the matt linen weave.

DOOR CURTAINS

I like to leave my doors wide open on warm sunny days to filter strong breezes. The calico curtains tie to the same poles which hold my winter curtains. For fun, I embroidered them with the name of our house.

Door curtains are essential in most country homes for the winter months to rebuff the coldness from the window glass and to prevent the prevailing wind sneaking its way round door frames. Interline with heavy bump and use substantial fabrics for both front fabric and lining. Make curtains overlong so that they just sweep the floor. Give them double hems that can be let down and used to replace the first hem as it wears after a few years of constant rubbing on the floor.

Internal door curtains are also sometimes useful to temper draughts in winter or to dress a doorless opening.

At the back of my house there is a small area which always catches the early morning sun, making it an ideal spot for breakfast. The only drawback is that it opens on to the main garden, catching any westerly breeze. Instead of opening and closing the garden gate, I hang a patchwork curtain in the summer to keep the eating area draught-free. You could make a similar curtain with any patchwork pieces from your fabric box, arranging bits from old curtains, cushions and clothes creating a very personal melange.

Regular guests have been surprised to find the same curtain serving as a very acceptable single bedcover later in the year!

MAKING UP

My lovely patchwork 'door' curtain is made from pieces collected over the years. Just remember to check that any scraps you gather for this project are washable at the same temperature.

1. Cut squares of equal sizes and pin to a calico ground. Stitch each in place with a long tacking stitch.

2. Position cotton tape to cover all raw edges and stitch in place. Bind the outer edges with more tape and stitch cut lengths to the heading to tie the curtain on to hooks or a pole.

DESIGN AND MAKE CURTAINS

1. When I found this fabric for my new curtains I thought it would be fun to make a flat door curtain. You could adapt this idea to curtain the doors from a beach house or pool changing room, using towelling or deck-chair fabric. Or try a waterproof fabric in place of a shower door. It is also the perfect solution, in almost any fabric, for covering open shelves or alcoves.

Using three complementary fabrics or two fabrics and a binding tape, cut two pieces which fit the doorway exactly and two pieces for the flap, approximately 70 cm (28 in) deep. Pin the pieces together with right sides out. Bind both panels around the two sides and hem. Join together at the top. Stitch fabric ties to hold the two together. Fit a narrow metal bar into the door recess and slot the curtain over.

2. Often there is only space to one side of a doorway, so a curtain must be made and fitted to pull from one direction to completely cover the opening. A simple wooden holdback contains this curtain when the door is in use.

3. Door curtains in a restricted space need to be tied back to allow the door to open freely. I have one narrow curtain which pulls to the opening side of the door and a wider one pulling back to the hinged side.

4. A heavy Italian chenille bedcover at the end of a corridor leading to a guest room can be looped back or dropped down to close off the corridor without the barrier of a solid door.

1

2

3

4

CONTRAST LININGS

Simple ideas using fabric in a stylish way are often the most effective. I love the way that the simple gingham check opens to reveal fabric which would usually have been used for the front.

I almost always line curtains with a contrasting fabric, rather than the normal creams and ecrus. However, I rarely use a plain colour, which may be too strong viewed from outside, preferring instead simple stripes and two-coloured small prints which add to the overall design rather than making a statement. The element of surprise and delight when the curtains are pulled back to reveal another unexpected dimension is an additional pleasure.

Choosing two patterns to work so closely together can take much time and research, but when they work as well as this combination does, the time was more than well spent. The secret is to choose a complementary fabric which reflects something of the main fabric, while at the same time bringing in another dimension. When I designed the curtaining shown on page 71, I was thrilled to find such a perfect fabric for the lining, at once echoing the spirit of the toile and introducing the perfect cottage garden flowers threaded through the finest blue pinstripe.

The scallops, opposite, were cut using a template, but left uneven to look 'hand cut'. They were then edged with blanket stitch in embroidery thread, which is so simple but looks so very effective.

Where the linings are intended to be on show, the edges need to be finished neatly. One way to do this is to finish the edge with cord or piping. This piping (below) was chosen to pick up the main greeny blue colour, stitched to the lining before making up.

Checks and stripes always make pleasing combinations. Richly coloured curtains in browns and reds are bordered in a plain caramel and lined with a terracotta stripe (above right). The interlining is locked to the curtain fabric and the lining to the inter-lining before the binding is stitched on. The binding strips are pinned to the front and stitched on, through all layers, pressed,

folded to the back and hand stitched to cover the stitching line. The instructions on page 9 for binding edgings will help you. Before you take the curtain off the worktable, pin all around at about 5 cm (2 in) intervals with the pins at right angles to the edges. These pins will remain in place while the binding is stitched on, keeping the fabrics together and the lining straight.

Helpful reference

Interlined curtains page 22, bound edgings page 9, inverted pleat headings page 29.

Door curtains are often seen from both sides, in which case equal attention needs to be given to both fabrics. Fabrics that are very similar in weight and coordinate as perfectly as these do, look stunning, but you could use lighter and darker colourings and, with the right headings, make the curtain reversible for winter and summer.

MAKING UP

Neatening the edge

If curtains are equally valid from both sides, as in the case of room dividers, bed curtains and door curtains, each fabric should be stitched together right on the edge to create a neat finish. Stitching piping, cording, or fringing to either side neatens the edge and provides an anchor against which to stitch the other side.

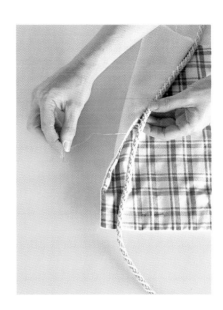

Adding piping

A piped edge stitched to the lining before making up gives a firm line to stitch against and looks impressive.

Cut linings 3 cm (1¼ in) smaller all round than the flat curtain. Stitch piping to the sides and hem, place lining on to the curtain, lock in and stitch to the main fabric with small, neat running stitches through the back of the piping.

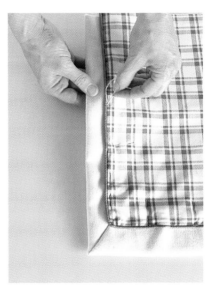

Patterned lining

Using a plain fabric on the front of a curtain and a patterned one on the inside can be very effective. To achieve this, the headings must remain in position while the curtains are held back. This lets the light shine through to show up the patterned lining.

Take the lining around to the front to make a narrow binding. Mitre the corner, as shown. Slip stitch the binding in place, just catching a thread from the lining side of the curtain.

BORDERS AND EDGINGS

Plain damask weave cotton is enhanced with an inset contrasting border and finished with fabric-covered buttons and ties. The under-curtains were first edged with a coordinating checked fabric before a linen cut fringe was stitched between the curtain and the lining.

It goes without saying that the edgings you choose will dramatically affect the style of your window treatment. Attention to the detailed finish of any curtaining will optimise the hard work which you have put in so far, and whether a simple binding or an elaborate fringe, the right edging will bring the fabric to life, enriching a wool damask, defining an all-over print or redefining a slubbed cotton.

There are so many different possibilities for edgings that you might find it difficult to make a choice – straight, frilled, double, single, on one side or four sides, buttoned, braided, scalloped, and so on. Curtains may appear harder or softer, more elegant or more informal, more contemporary or more traditional, depending on the style and colours of the edgings.

A formal room might suggest elegant passementerie while a contemporary setting demands a structured shape and defined lines. If you are as yet unsure how your other furnishings will take shape, it would be prudent to select an edging which subtly complements the main fabric as opposed to one which might prove to be too overpowering later on.

Consider the ways in which you might mix fringes and bindings, double or inset borders, braids with frills, a checked border against a traditional print, using large checks with small checks, large prints with small prints, but always choosing fabrics of a similar weight and content, so that both cloths will react to atmospheric changes in the same way.

BINDINGS AND BORDERS

Adding bindings and borders to curtains gives you the opportunity to experiment with different colours and textures. Borders may be wide, narrow, on the edge, or set in from the edge, and on as many sides of the curtain as you wish. Double and triple borders take time and need very accurate cutting and stitching but are always most effective. Try using one or two plain colours set into a pattern.

The really important factor to consider is that the fabrics must be of similar quality and content. It would be such a shame to have spent time choosing and making to find the fabrics reacting differently to room temperature and pulling against each other. So a matt finish may be used with a sheen, pattern with plain, stripe with pattern, as long as the fibre content is the same and the weave similar.

The closely co-ordinated colours of the double curtains and edgings on page 57 are harmonious and quietly elegant.

MAKING BOUND EDGES

My standard edging size is 1.5 cm (⅝ in). I often adjust this a fraction either way, slightly more for a larger curtain or a deeper frill, and less for a dark colour or smaller frill. Order edging fabric to be at least as long as your curtains, so that the strips can be cut the length of the roll, entailing as few joins as possible, with none at all on the leading edge.

EDGING AN UNLINED CURTAIN

1. Cut and join enough strips of fabric 6 cm (2¼ in) wide to bind all edges.

2. Place the curtain flat on to the worktable with the wrong side facing down. Pin the edging strip along the leading edge as shown. Stop pinning 1.5 cm (⅝ in) from the corner. Fold the edging over at a right angle and continue pinning along the hemline.

3. Stitch along the leading edge at exactly 1.4 cm (just under ⅝ in) from the raw edges. Stop stitching 1.5 cm (⅝ in) from the hem edge at the corner point. Fold the flap over and start stitching again at the other side of the flap, checking that the needle is inserted next to the last stitch.

These simple curtains made from ticking have been bound on all four edges with a deep yellow cotton to echo the colours of the ties and window seat.

DESIGN AND MAKE CURTAINS

4. From the right side, press the edging strip away from the curtain. Fold back under 1.5 cm (⅝ in), folding the edging tight against the seam, mitre the corner.

5. Turn the fabric over to the back. Mitre the corner by first folding the free side to the curtain edge and over again to enclose the raw edges. Snip the adjacent binding strip towards the corner, and fold the next length of binding over as before. Pin to hold in place. Slip stitch every 1 cm (⅜ in), picking up a machine stitch as you go so that no stitches are visible from the front.

BINDING A LINED CURTAIN

Follow the method above, but lock stitch the lining to the main fabric first and tack round all the edges to hold the pieces together.

BINDING AN INTERLINED CURTAIN

1. Cut and join enough strips of fabric 11 cm (4¼ in) wide, to bind all edges.

2. Place the curtain fabric on to the worktable and trim away the selvedge. If your curtains are small and you are using lightweight interlining, lock stitch the interlining to the curtain fabric and treat as one piece. Pin the binding to the curtain edge from the heading towards the hem. Stop pinning 9.5 cm (3½ in) from the hem. Fold the edging over at a right angle and continue pinning parallel with the hem.

3. Stitch along the leading edge exactly 1.4 cm (just under ⅝ in) from the raw edge. It is important that the stitching line is very accurate to give an even edging. Stop at the corner 9.5 cm (3½ in) from the hem edge and secure the stitching. Fold the flap over and continue to stitch along the other side, starting 1.5 cm (⅝ in) from the leading edge. The stitches should meet at the corner.

4. Working from the front, press the binding away from the curtain. Fold the binding to the back of the curtain, measuring from the front 1.5 cm (⅝ in) all along as you pin. Carefully mitre the corner at the front.

5. Fold over and mitre the back corner. Trim the binding on the leading edge only to 6 cm (2¼ in), leaving the hem.

Continue to make up the curtain following instructions on pages 24-25 stitching the lining to leave 1.5 cm (⅝ in) of the edging visible.

6. Herringbone stitch the hem and long stitch the sides to the interlining. Continue to make curtains following the instructions on pages 24-25, stitching the lining and leaving just 1.5 cm (⅝ in) visible.

MAKING AN INSET BORDER

The strips of fabric to make an inset border need to be cut 3 cm (1¼ in) wider than the finished border width. The outer border, or binding, should be cut to twice the finished width plus 3 cm (1¼ in). Cut and join enough strips to complete the edgings.

1. Place the curtain on the work-table, wrong side down, and pin the inset strips to the side, starting at the heading. Stop 1.5 cm (⅝ in) from the hem and fold the edging back on itself, allowing enough fabric so the border is mitred when finished. Continue pinning 1.5 cm (⅝ in) from the side edge. Repeat with other side. Stitch in place keeping 1.5 cm (⅝ in) from the raw edges.

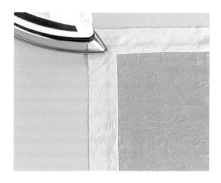

2. Press from the front, away from the curtain. Press on the back, snipping along the short fold so that it lies flat.

3. With right sides together, pin the outside edging strip to the inset strip, mitring the corners as before. Stitch 1.5 cm (⅝ in) from the raw edges. Press from the front, away from the curtain and fold the edging under. Pin in place, turn over and mitre the corner.

4. Turn the fabric over and mitre the back corner, folding the border fabric in the opposite direction to keep the corner as flat as possible.

BOUGHT EDGINGS

Fringing, ribbons, cord and braids are readily available from furnishing fabric suppliers and department stores and they are an excellent way of edging your curtains quickly. Take a sample piece of fabric with you when shopping to ensure a good tonal match or contrast. Bear in mind the weight of fabric you are using and how the edging will be attached. Make sure you buy slightly more than slightly less, as the exact colour and style of edgings bought later may not match up.

1. I wanted the fringe to be less important on these under-curtains, so I stitched it behind a narrow border cut on the cross.

Adding a fringe to the leading edge of a curtain can make any fabric look elegant. Some fringes have decorative tops which ask to be shown, so these are best stitched to the front. Others have very plain tops and should be stitched between the top fabric and the lining.

Choose a linen or cotton fringe for linen or cotton fabrics and silk or a silky fibre for silk and damask fabrics.

2. I think ribbons will be taken much more seriously as a decorative detail in the next few years. I use ribbon for piping, for ties, or for binding edges. Plain or decorative ribbons are available in a vast selection of widths and colours, from matt ribbed hat ribbon to lustrous gold and silver creations

with wired edges which can be moulded into any shape, including the most marvellous bows. Embroidered cotton and linen ribbons are lovely for bedlinen and cushions as well as the leading edges of curtains.

3. Fan topped and fan edged braidings make particularly smart edgings for curtains, pelmets and cushions and are available in many colour combinations from interior decorators and furnishing fabric suppliers. I designed this jumbo fanned edging with my client especially for these hand-worked crewel curtains. A small passementerie company made up the edging together with matching cord which I used for cushions and tiebacks.

4. A coloured cord, hand-stitched to the edges and hems, adds a subtle finish to any curtain. Buy dainty 4–6 mm ($\frac{1}{8}$–$\frac{1}{4}$ in) cord for lightweight curtains and up to 20 mm ($\frac{1}{2}$ in) cord for the heaviest wools and woven tapestries. Use contrasting colours for a smart finish, say red with navy, or related colours for a subtle finish such as apricot with soft pink. To make this padded edge, inset a roll of interlining all round before stitching the sides and hems in place. Stitch right through to the front to really secure the roll and stitch the cord to cover.

BORDERS ON THE CROSS

Instead of selecting a contrasting or complementary fabric for the borders, use the same fabric. Why not turn checks crosswise, cut stripes on the cross or in the opposite direction, or design a border cut in the same direction but with braiding between.

I designed the curtains opposite for a bedroom decorated only in red checks in varying scales. I wanted to add a border which was subtle enough not to become the focal point, but interesting enough to add another dimension. Cutting the fabric on the cross provided the diversion; brown ribbon details the change.

A simple unlined curtain in blue checked cotton would not be nearly as interesting without the cross cut borders (right). Jumbo piping covered with checked lining fabric cut on the cross provides a neat edge to these fun kitchen curtains (below).

MAKING UP

1. Cut the borders for the sides and hems across the grain of the fabric 12 cm (4¾ in) wide and for the heading 22 cm (8¾ in) wide. Place the ribbon along one edge of the right side of each border and stitch neatly in place, halfway across the ribbon width.

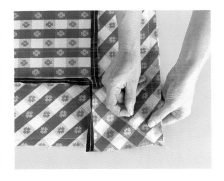

2. Pin the borders to the sides and hem with right sides facing and stitch with a 1.5 cm (⅝ in) seam. Pin across the corners to mitre and stitch.

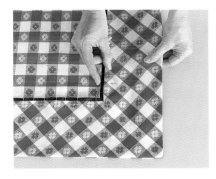

3. Press the seam flat and trim across the corner. Turn the border to the right side and press the seam lines. Press one half of the ribbon underneath the border and pin this edge flat on to the curtains to create a neat, even trim.

4. Stitch the border in place neatly along the edge of the ribbon trim.

5. To make the attached pelmet, line the heading border and pin to the curtains with right sides together. Make ties 1.5 × 60 cm (⅝ × 24 in) following the instructions on page 8. Insert in pairs and stitch the ties and border to the curtain securely, neaten the seam and fold the border to the front of the curtain.

FRILLED EDGES

One of my favourite commissions was a delightful Queen Anne house which was decorated with such attention to detail that it always reminds me of a grown-up dolls' house. Every item has been positioned perfectly and every edging designed to the last detail.

It interests me that in two dictionaries I find the word frill expounded as 'unnecessary ornament' and as a 'treat, bauble, delicacy'. This seems to sum up exactly how frilled edgings might fit into a design scheme. Frills are often completely unnecessary and could spoil the line; however, for some window treatments, frills are essential to make the design work. It is never right to frill everything, but often the effect of frills edging curtains or cushions does provide the 'treat' – the icing on the cake.

Frilled edgings are an extravagance, taking time and a considerable amount of extra fabric, but they do offer a softer look to curtains and drapes than more formal edgings and bindings. The opportunity for mixing fabrics and colours adds a fun element to the design process. Use magazines, books, shop windows, colour charts, small samples and scraps of fabrics for ideas. Balancing the scale of prints is essential – look carefully at the fabrics you plan to put together – you might need to alter the width of a stripe, the size of a check or the scale of a pattern for the perfect combination. Be careful that one colour or pattern does not overwhelm the others, and keep colourings within the same tonal range. Or you might prefer to make a strong statement, in which case, keep within the same tonal range, perhaps mixing forest green and deep terracotta red; or use one colour with a neutral – navy blue with white.

Overlong frills can be very effective – a 20 cm (8 in) frill stitched to the leading edge and hem and tied back tightly so that the frills fall with the drape, makes a different but equally strong statement.

DESIGN AND MAKE CURTAINS

BOUND AND BACKED FRILLS

1. Cut and join strips of fabric, allowing twice the overall drop of each curtain, 9 cm (3½ in) wide for the frill fabric and 12 cm (4¾ in) for the binding and backing. Pin each strip together, right sides facing and stitch along the length, 1.5 cm (⅝ in) from the edge. From the front, press the 12 cm (4¾ in) strip away from the narrower strip. Press under and pin, keeping an exact 1.5 cm (⅝ in) edging.

2. Fold under each end by 1.5 cm (⅝ in) stitch together with small ladder stitches. Run a gathering thread along the length 1.5 cm (⅝ in) from the raw edges. Measure the exact frill length, divide into 10 equal sections and mark with coloured marking tacks.

3. Pipe the leading edge of the curtain following the instructions on page 9. Divide the piped edge into 10 equal sections and mark with coloured marking tacks. Pull up the gathering thread and pin together, matching the section tacks. Spread the gathers evenly between as you go.

4. Stitch the frill to the piping line, keeping just inside the first stitching line. Trim the seam and layer to reduce the bulk if necessary. Herringbone stitch the piping and frilled edge to the main fabric or interlining. Slip stitch the lining close to the piping cord to enclose all raw edges.

SCALLOPED FRILLED HEMS

Create a template (see page 68) to make scallops along the curtain hemline, allowing 4–5 for each width of fabric. If the curtains are interlined, lock stitch the main fabric and interlining together and make up as one. Make piping (page 9) and stitch around the scallops, 1.5 cm (⅝ in) from the cut edge. Carefully snip into the points.

The attached skirt falls level with the floor so it needs to be shaped to fit the curtain scalloped edge before making up. I used scallops which measured 25 cm wide × 8 cm deep (10 × 3¼ in)

Lilac and yellow as a sophisticated colour combination translates equally well into this classical toile print, depicting scenes of traditional Chinese life. Glazed lilac linen has been used for the skirt and a small yellow ochre check to pipe the scallops. Sofas in lilac, piped with the same yellow check, with toile cushions echo the window treatment.

and allowed double fullness for
gathering the skirt.

Divide the lined frill into 50 cm
(20 in) sections and cut 8 cm
(3¼ in) deep scallops, using the
first template as a guide. Run a
gathering thread 1.5 cm (⅝ in)
from the raw edge, pull up and

pin to the piping line, spreading
the gathers evenly into each
section. Stitch close to the piping
line and neaten the raw edges.

Do this with binding tape if the
curtain is to be unlined, or slip
stitch the lining to enclose the
whole seam, if lined.

**A pretty courtyard outlook needed
curtains which would rarely be drawn,
but would frame the window in a style
compatible with the rest of the house. I
decided to tie and drape these curtains
high up away from the sink and other
utensils., choosing another colourway
of the same fabric to line and edge.**

SCALLOPED EDGINGS

The window treatment opposite combines matt silk with a fine Italian cotton printed in a traditional paisley design. The paisley border has been joined to the leading edge with fine soft lemon cord, and a scalloped border in matt silk has been joined to the paisley border and hem, also with the cord. These curtains are shown over-long with the hems fanned out. Curtain headings are hand gathered in pencil pleats, with attached pelmets of paisley squares gathered up and stitched to hold. I have often used silk scarves for similar treatments.

Over-long curtains in crushed raspberry and caramel – with bold scallops – make an unusual but effective colour combination for an informal dining room, whether to accompany contemporary or traditional furnishings.

MAKING SCALLOPS

For the best effect, scallops should all be even in size and the best way to achieve this accurately, is to make a template using stiff paper and a round object like a saucer or the lid of a jar.

1. Cut a piece of card or a strip of heading buckram the length of the curtain and mark it into sections for each scallop. Also mark the depth of the scallop at the widest and narrowest points. Draw around a household object – like a saucer or bowl – to define the first shape. Trace this one and use it to repeat the shape. Cut out the template with scissors.

2. Pin this template on to the main fabric and draw round it.

3. Cut the scalloped edges, leaving 1 cm (³⁄₈ in) seam allowance all round. Cut a strip of fabric for the facing which is the length of the curtain × the depth of the scallop. Pin the facing to the curtain, right sides together. Stitch around the scallops, keeping the stitching line an even 1 cm (³⁄₈ in) from the raw edge. Trim seams and snip right into the points. Snip the curves as close to the stitching as possible so that they will lie flat when turned.

4. Turn out and press the scallops into even, rounded shapes. Continue to make up your curtains, lining or interlining as pages 18–25.

5. If the scalloped edge is to be a border to a curtain, in either a contrasting fabric or colour, you might like to pipe the curtain all round first. Always mitre the corners correctly.

PELMETS

If you want to use toile de jouy, use it everywhere. These two fabrics looked so good together that we almost had a problem choosing which was to be the curtain and which the lining. Doubled unlined pelmets trimmed in a hand-made picot edging are cut to perfection and seem to be as French as the fabric.

Pelmets provide the ultimate finishing touch to a window treatment; however, they can take as long to make as the curtains themselves and can cost much more if you indulge in elaborate trimmings and details.

Look at interiors magazines and books for ideas which might be compatible with your window style. Check out the latest fabrics and trimmings and the way in which fashion is influencing furnishings design. Nothing is ever absolutely *de rigueur* as it might be with say, a hemline, but there are certainly trends and details which can make all the difference between a successful and a mediocre window treatment.

Pelmets should, almost without exception, start from the ceiling and must always be deep enough to cover the window frame and any unsightly fittings. Double glazing, blind and security fittings are the worst offenders.

The rule of thumb for pelmet depth is an average of one-fifth on the curtain drop. This might be a good place to start, but use it as a guide rather than a rule; the ideas picked up from interiors magazines are probably just as reliable.

DESIGN AND MAKE CURTAINS

SWAGGED PELMETS

Swags and tails have become so much part of elegant period window treatments that I am often asked to explain how to make them. But to be able to cut and drape good swags takes an experienced curtain maker some time to learn and there are no short cuts to training and experience. I do teach experienced makers to design, drape and cut over a four day course, but as this time is not possible for most people I have adapted a very simple principle to show you how to make an elegant pelmet without draping.

It is still important that the numbers, depth and shape of the swags are well balanced. Have a pelmet board made which is 10 cm (4 in) deep (see page 12) and fit it in position. Drape and pin a length of chain or chain weight across the board to determine the swag sizes. Try out two or three swags on a pelmet board of up to 1.8 m (6 ft) wide and three or five after that.

When you are happy with the pelmet design, measure the drape and the distance along the board for the top of each swag, and the drape. Measure the depth of each swag. Add 4 cm (1½ in) to the width measurements and two and a half times the depth. Cut out one piece of fabric, mediumweight inter-lining and lining for each swag.

I use large thumb tacks to pin swags to pelmet boards. These are

easy to fit and simple to remove when the swags need shaking out or cleaning. Often there is only enough space between the board and ceiling to just fit two fingers and a thumb tack.

To make a very simple under swag, measure the depth from the pelmet board to the hemline of the

under swag and cut a semi-circle to this diameter. Leave unlined or line with the same lining used for the pelmets. Make three pleats across the top, with one central pleat, and stitch to a flat band. Finish the lower edge with fringe or braiding, or leave plain and fit to the pelmet.

MAKING UP

1. Make one swag at a time. Place one piece of fabric on to the worktable, right side down. Shape the lower edge to curve slightly from approximately 3 cm (1¼ in) on each side. Place the interlining on top and lock in approximately three times across the swag.

2. Trim away 2 cm (¾ in) of interlining from the sides and hem. Stitch the interlining to the fabric around the three sides with herringbone stitch.

3. Fold over the main fabric, press lightly, pin and herringbone to the interlining. Place the lining over and lock in along the previous lines.

4. With the point of your scissors, score the lining around the folded edges of the swag. Trim the lining 1 cm (⅜ in) outside this line. Fold under 2 cm (¾ in) and pin to the swag, leaving 1 cm (⅜ in) of the swag fabric showing.

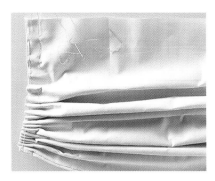

5. Slip stitch all round. Now thread two large needles with double thread longer than the swag. Start from the hemline and secure the thread 1 cm (⅜ in) from one side and 3 cm (1¼ in) further in. Stitch the two threads parallel to each other, with exactly the same stitch size to the top. Experiment with the stitch size – longer stitches will give deeper pleats, small stitches will look like gathering. Here, I used stitches showing 1 cm (⅜ in) on the lining and 2.5 cm (1 in) in front.

6. Repeat with the other side. Pull up both sides and secure the threads. If you are using a rosette or rose to finish the centre, pull up tightly. Cover a 5 cm (2 in) strip of heading tape with fabric and stitch to the top edge to enclose the raw edges. Pin the swags to the pelmet board with thumb tacks.

GATHERED PELMETS

Whether you have chosen to make a flat or a gathered pelmet you should always start from a basic template. Think of it in the same manner as a tailor's dummy over which you may drape, pleat and gather to your heart's content. A professional curtain maker might allow several hours to perfect a pelmet shape, so do not try or expect to rush this process. Time and care in preparation always show in the end result.

To make a template, stand back from your window and mark the wall or frame with a light pencil where you imagine the centre and sides will fall. Translate these measurements on to brown paper or newspaper, draw your design within them and cut out. Pin the template to the frame or wall along the top line. Stand back and pretend you are taller and shorter than you are so that you know what other people see. Adjust the template until you are happy with the shape.

Bowed pelmets emphasise the serpentine-shaped pelmet hem. Fancy lining and matching fan edging pick up the pink flowers from the chintz.

MAKING UP

1. Using a metal ruler, set square and a thick pencil, mark one half of the template into divisions. Use 4–5 cm (½–2in) spacing where there is little shaping and 2–3 cm (¾–1¼ in) divisions where there is more shaping. Number these divisions and cut into strips.

2. Make a toile in calico or spare fabric before cutting expensive fabric. Cut and join scrap fabric to the finished depth and three times the length of your template and clamp it to the worktable. Starting at the centre, place the paper strips parallel to the centre line, leaving gaps in between to create fullness. Two and a half times fullness is average, so leave 4.5 cm (1¾ in) for each 3 cm (1¼ in) paper strip. Add the pelmet board return and equivalent fullness.

3. When all the pieces are in place, cut around the lower edge, following the lowest point of each piece, and cut the return so that the hem line runs smoothly.

4. Fold the fabric in half and cut the other half to match. Run a large gathering thread through the pelmet approximately 6 cm (2¼ in) from the top and pull up to the template size. Fit to the window to check the shaping and make any adjustments. Pleat the gathers evenly and 'dress' the toile as if it were the real thing, remembering that the hem line will be weighted with trimmings or bindings and that the fabric will be of a superior quality to the toile.

5. From the template, plan the fabric cuts so that there is always a full width in the centre and part widths at either side. Cut out and join linings and interlinings to fit, but without the shaping.

6. Place the pelmet face down with the interlining over and lock stitch at 30 cm (12 in) intervals. Trim the interlining to shape around the lower edge.

7. If you are binding the lower edge, pin and stitch 1.5 cm (⅝ in) in from the raw edge. Press from the right side and fold neatly back to the wrong side. Herringbone stitch in place.

If binding is not being used, turn the sides and hem under 2 cm (¾ in) and press. Unfold and trim away the interlining. Fold the hem back and herringbone stitch.

8. Place the lining over and lock stitch to the interlining along the same lines. Score the lining along the edge of the pelmet fold and trim 1 cm (⅜ in) from this line. Fold hem under 1.5 cm (⅝ in) and slip stitch to the pelmet.

9. Tidy up the top edge if necessary. Measure from the top and turn over the heading allowance. Trim away any interlining and complete the headings.

UPHOLSTERED PELMETS

Upholstered pelmets are making something of a come-back after the excess of frills and chintzes in the last few years. Traditionally, flat pelmets would have been made with formal fabrics – damasks, brocades, velvets, and decorated with cords and braids. Unbleached linens and country stripes or plain cottons are contemporary alternatives.

Mix a strong, striped fabric on the pelmet with plain curtains, or use a floral chintz for the pelmet over plain curtains bordered in the same chintz. Woven or tapestry lambrequins, found in antiques shops or markets, can sometimes be adapted and reshaped to fit around a window. An elaborate pelmet with detailed fabric and trimmings could be used on its own with perhaps a blind or shutters beneath.

You will need to follow the instructions on page 15 to make up a flat template in a pleasing shape. Or you might prefer to draw the window on to graph paper, marking the centre and side depths, and designing your pelmet to accommodate these.

Scale up the design to full size on to brown paper. Cut out and fit on to the window frame. Check that the design is correct from all angles, and add or take away sections until you are satisfied with the result. Plan the fabric required.

MAKING UP

1. Cut, join and press the fabric and lining, remembering to use a full width of fabric at the centre. Cut out the interlining. Cut the pelmet from wood or pelmet buckram.

2. Spread a thin layer of glue over the front of the pelmet, place the interlining over the top, smoothing it out as you work. Carefully trim away any excess.

3. Place the main fabric on to the worktable, face downwards. Pin to the table and place the pelmet over the top, interlining side down. Line up seams and keep at right angles to the straight edge. Trim the fabric to 3.5 cm (1⅜ in) all round the edge of the pelmet. Spread glue around the edges and fold the main fabric over.

4. Place the lining over the pelmet and pin around the edge to hold. Score along the pelmet edge with the point of your scissors and trim the lining 2 cm (¾ in) from this mark. Fold along the scored line and pin to the pelmet edge. Stitch the lining to the main fabric with a curved upholstery needle.

5. Slip stitch cord to the lower edge so that the lining is not visible from the front and stitch the fitting tape to the top edge.

At the bottom of each side, hand stitch small tabs which will be pinned into the window frame or wall to prevent the pelmet moving. Stitch heading tape or touch and close tape just below the top line. A deep pelmet should have two or three rows to hold it.

Fit to the pelmet board with large drawing pins through the heading tape or to the opposite side of the touch and close tape.

FLAT PELMETS

Cotton huckaback – used for commercial handtowels, mattress ticking and denim – proves that effective window treatments do not need to cost a great deal. The pelmet is simply a triangle of fabric, with the top fabric cut 10 cm (4 in) smaller and the lining 14 cm (5½ in) larger, piped and hand stitched over the smaller triangle. The long side of the triangle measures from the bottom of the 'dropped sides' and over the pelmet board.

The pelmet drape could have been hung over a pole and pulled up in the centre, caught in place with another piece of fabric.

CURTAIN CARE

Washing / cleaning

Unlined curtains are usually made when regular cleaning will be needed and should be washed or dry cleaned in accordance with the manufacturer's instructions. If frequent washing is essential, use a strong, hardwearing fabric, such as cotton, with enough substance to stand regular handling. To prevent shrinkage, either wash the fabric before making it up or over-cut the drops and make up the curtains with the shrinkage allowance so that this will be taken up at the first wash.

Make sure that every trace of detergent is removed. Sunlight can react with cleaning chemicals and cause fading. Always press while still damp, as pressing and steaming will keep fabric in shape. Try not to press over seams, only press up to them with the point of the iron. If you do need to press over a seam, slip a piece of cloth between the seam and the main fabric to prevent a ridge forming.

Airing

The best and most effective way to keep curtains clean and fresh is to choose a slightly breezy day, open the windows wide, close the curtains and allow them to blow in the breeze for a few hours. This will remove the slightly musty lining smell. If you can do this every few weeks your curtains will always stay fresh. This is more of a problem in the city, but is possible if you choose quiet, breezy spring and autumn Sundays.

Vacuuming

The regular removal of dust is vital to prevent particles of household dust settling into the fabric grain, as once dirt has penetrated it is very difficult and often impossible to remove with any satisfaction.

Vacuum all soft furnishings regularly with a soft brush, paying special attention to the inside of chair seats, pleats and frills. For delicate fabrics and pelmets make a muslin or fine calico 'mob cap', elasticated to fit over the end of the brush to soften the bristle/fabric abrasion.

Dry cleaning

Small furnishings, eg silk cushions, will need to be dry cleaned at regular intervals, so use a specialist furnishings dry cleaner and clean before dirt is ingrained.

Clean interlined curtains only when disaster strikes or before alterations. Regular care and attention will prevent curtains from becoming 'dirty'.

Alterations

If curtains need to be altered for any reason (like moving house) have them cleaned by a specialist dry cleaner before alterations are carried out. Remove stitching from the sides and hems to allow any ruckled fabric to be cleaned and to allow the fabrics to shrink at different rates.

Track maintenance

Periodically spray the inside of curtain track and the top of poles with an anti-static household cleaner or silicone spray to prevent dust building up and to ease the running.

Poles may be cleaned with a dilute household cleaner and a soft brush to remove dust from the crevices of decorative finials and the underside of curtain pole rings.

GLOSSARY

FIBRES

Acrylic Manmade from petrol, often mixed with more expensive fibres to keep the cost down. Not hardwearing, but useful for permanent pleating.

Cotton A natural fibre, cotton is very versatile, woven, knitted and mixed with other fibres. Used for any soft furnishings according to weight. It will lose strength in direct sunlight, so protect. Soft, strong, easy to launder, washable if pre-shrunk.

Linen Fibres found inside the stalks of the flax plant are woven to make linen cloth in almost any weight. Distinctive slub weave from very fine linen for under-curtains and sheers to heavy upholstery weight. A very strong fibre which is easy to work and will take high temperatures.

Silk From the cocoon of the silk worm, silk is soft and luxurious to touch. Fades in sunlight, so protect. Available in every weight, suitable for soft furnishings, from lampshades to heavy upholstery. Good mixed with cotton or wool.

Wool A natural fibre, liable to excessive shrinkage as the 'scales' on each fibre overlap, harden and 'felt'. Is warm to touch and initially resists damp. Ideal for upholstery and curtains.

Viscose Wood pulp woven into fibres which mixes well with other fibres helping them to take dyes and fireproofing. Washable and sheds dirt easily.

FABRICS

Brocade Traditionally woven fabric using silk, cotton, wool or mixed fibres, on a jacquard loom, in a multi or self coloured floral design. Brocades drape well and can be used for curtains, traditional bed drapes, covers and upholstery. Some are washable but most will need dry cleaning.

Calico Coarse, plain weave cotton in cream or white with 'natural' flecks in it. Available in many widths and weights for inexpensive curtains, bed drapes, garden awnings. Wash before use to shrink and press while damp.

Cambric Closely woven, plain weave fabric from linen or cotton with a sheen on one side. Use, wash and press as Calico. Widely used for cushion pad covers but also for curtains, covers and cushions.

Canvas Plain weave cotton in various weights suitable for upholstered chair covers, inexpensive curtains, slip covers, awnings and outdoor use. Available as unbleached, coarse cotton or more finely woven and dyed in strong colours.

Chintz Cotton fabric with Eastern design using flowers and birds, often with a resin finish which gives a characteristic sheen or glaze and which also repels dirt. The glaze will eventually wash out, so only dry clean curtains. Avoid using steam to press and never fold or the glaze will crack.

Corduroy A strong fabric woven to form vertical ribs by floating extra yarn across which is then cut to make the pile. Use for traditional upholstery. Press on a velvet pinboard while damp.

Crewel Plain or hopsack woven, natural cotton background embroidered in chain stitch in plain cream wool or multi-coloured wools. Soft but heavy, lovely for curtains, soft blinds, cushions and light-use loose covers. May be washed, but test a small piece first.

Damask A jacquard fabric first woven in Damascus with satin floats on a warp satin background in cotton, silk, wool and mixed fibres in various weights. Use for curtains, drapes and sometimes covers and upholstery, choosing different weights for different uses. Make up reversed if a matt finish is required. Suitable for curtaining which needs to be seen from both sides.

Gingham Plain weave fabric with equal width stripes of white plus one other colour in both warp and weft threads to produce blocks of checks or stripes in 100% cotton. Use for small windows in cottagey rooms, kitchens, children's bedrooms and slip covers. Mix with floral patterns and other checks and stripes.

Holland Firm, hardwearing fabric made from cotton or linen stiffened with oil or shellac. Used for blinds lightweight covers, curtaining and pelmets.

Lace Open work fabrics in designs ranging from simple spots to elaborate panels. Usually in cotton or a cotton and polyester mixture.

Moiré A finish usually on silk or acetate described as 'watermarked'. The characteristic moiré markings are produced by pressing plain woven fabric through hot engraved cylinders which crush the threads and push them into different directions to form the pattern. This finish will disappear on contact with water, so it is not suitable for upholstery.

Muslin White or off-white, inexpensive, open-weave cloth which can be dyed in pastel colours. Used for under-curtains and sheers in hot countries to filter light and insects.

Organdie The very finest cotton fabric with an acid finish giving it a unique crispness. Use for lightweight curtains, dressing tables and lampshades. Wash and press while damp.

Organza Similar to organdie and made of silk, polyester or viscose. Very springy and used for stiffening headings of fine fabrics, blinds to filter sunlight and to protect curtains. Use layers of varying tones or pastel colours over each other.

Provençal prints Small print designs printed by hand on to fine cotton for curtains, upholstery, cushions and covers. Washable, hard wearing, soft and easy to work with.

Silk noil Light to mediumweight silk, relatively inexpensive for interlining heavy curtains, slip covers, summer curtains and cushions.

Silk shantung Light to mediumweight silk woven with irregular yarns giving a dull, rough appearance. Use for curtains, cushions, light drapes and lampshades. Available in an extensive range of colours, gathers and frills.

Taffeta Woven from silk, acetate and blends. Used for elaborate drapes because it handles well and for its light-reflecting qualities.

Tartan Authentic tartans belong to individual Scottish clans and are woven or worsted fine twill weave with an elaborate checked design. Traditional wool tartans are hardwearing for upholstering sofas and chairs, curtains and cushions.

Ticking Characteristic original herringbone weave in black and white, now woven in many colours and weights. Use for curtains and upholstery. Not usually pre-shrunk.

Toile de jouy Pastoral designs in one colour printed on to calico using copper plate printing techniques. Use for curtains, covers, upholstery, cushions and bedding.

Tweed Wool or worsted cloth in square or rectangular checked designs in few colours. Often used for shawls or more tightly woven for men's sporting clothes. However, use for upholstering stools, chairs, sofas or for curtains, pelmets and cushions.

Velvet Originally 100% silk, now made from cotton, viscose or other manmade fibres. Woven with a warp pile and additional yarn in loops which are up to 3 mm (⅛ in) depth to form a pile. Care needs to be taken when sewing or the fabrics will 'walk'. Press on a velvet pinboard. Dry clean carefully. Always buy good quality velvet with a dense pile which will not pull out easily.

Voile Fine, light plain weave cotton or polyester fabric dyed in many plain colours. Use for filmy curtains, bed drapes and under-curtains. Easily washable and little pressing necessary. Silk and wool voiles can be used for fine drapery.

INDEX